BETTER RESUMES FOR COLLEGE GRADUATES

by
ADELE LEWIS
Former President and Founder
Career Blazers Agency, Inc.
New York City

BARRON'S EDUCATIONAL SERIES, INC.

All inquiries should be addressed to:
Barron's Educational Series, Inc.
250 Wireless Boulevard
Hauppauge, New York 11788

Library of Congress Catalog Card No. 84-28115

International Standard Book No. 0-8120-2701-9

Library of Congress Cataloging in Publication Data
Lewis, Adele Beatrice, 1927-
  Better resumes for college graduates.

  1. Résumés (Employment) 2. College graduates—
Employment. I. Title.
HF5383.L46   1985   650.1'4   84-28115
ISBN 0-8120-2701-9

PRINTED IN THE UNITED STATES OF AMERICA

1   100   9

Contents

Introduction

There is no feeling so devastating as the one that comes after a hard day of making the employment-agency rounds, dropping into the personnel departments of companies you'd love to work in—and still no decent job offer in sight. On the other hand, there is no feeling quite as exhilarating and triumphant as looking for a job and receiving several offers. Looking for a job for recent college graduates, as well as those high on the corporate ladder, can either be a triumph or a catastrophe, depending on one's expertise in the art of job hunting.

From long years of experience of working with college graduates seeking entry-level jobs, we've come to understand that the looking for and the getting of a job is a skill. It is a skill that can be learned, and once acquired will become a lifetime asset and forever remove any trepidation in regard to the job hunt.

It is our philosophy, for the college graduate looking for an *entry* level job, to *aim* for the best available, trying to avoid settling for less. But this must be tempered with a realistic attitude, evaluating each opportunity with a flexible and farsighted view. Examine each opportunity with "what can I learn," "is it promotable," "can I add something to that job which will make it more important to the company" or "how will it look on my résumé."

Be very careful *not* to be fooled by job titles. A secretary to an editor may very well be an editorial/assistant or editorial trainee, a Gal/Guy Friday in an advertising agency might really be the entry to a copywriting position, a secretary to an executive might be another name for an administrative assistant, a sales man or woman position can often be the stepping-stone to a marketing or management career. In essence, we're pointing out that not only jobs labeled *trainee* have potential.

It really is true that the companies prefer to train their own staff and promote from within. We've placed secretaries (not always with steno, but always with typing), both men and women who have become editors, publishers, account executives, television producers, production managers, writers, researchers, office managers, administrators, and vice-presidents.

Though we believe in holding out for the very best, we are also aware that a job is often what you make of it. We also believe that "Proximity is the Mother of Opportunity," so that an entry position in the field of your choice may very well be the first step to a successful career.

It is extremely important for the job seeker to maintain an optimistic, confident point of view. No matter what the economy, there are always jobs to be filled and companies are forever recruiting. If this were not so, the more than 5,000 employment agencies currently doing business in the United States would have to close their doors. In bad times, as well as good times, some of the vast majority of the employed retire, others relocate, others leave for personal reasons. Each time this happens, another job-to-be-filled opens. Our changing technology creates thousands of jobs which didn't exist twenty years ago, and even the fact that our population has a longer life span accounts for an increasing number of positions to be filled.

It is true that in times of an economic recession the recent college grad might have to try a little harder, but if he or she is willing to sustain an honest effort, possibly make certain compromises, and in some cases gain additional skills, the job hunt properly done is bound to be successful. Often, even in "bad" times the outcome of a successful job campaign results in several offers, and the problem changes from "how to find a job" to "which job do I take?"

The Perfect Job For You 1

The very first step in finding that "perfect" entry-level job is getting to know what you are looking for. Knowing where your talents lie, what you enjoy doing, and how that can be translated into a job title is the very guts of a successful job campaign. Knowledge of the job market, a dynamic résumé, superior contacts in the business world—all great assets in a job campaign—will not help you if you are basically unaware of your real interests and motivations.

Recent college graduates (especially those with a major in liberal arts) are surprisingly unsophisticated about the nature of entry-level jobs and very often extremely naïve when asked "what kind of job are you looking for?" A graduate with a degree in engineering is quite certain he or she is looking for an entry-level engineering job; likewise an accounting major is very straightforward in seeking a position in an accounting field. But those with majors in the humanities or liberal arts are not always quite sure where they fit in.

It is well worth the effort to spend a little time analyzing the inner you—discovering the situations in which you are the happiest, just exactly what turns you on. Socrates had a point when he said the basis of wisdom is self-knowledge and from that awareness all other knowledge can be acquired. It is obvious that it is impossible to understand anything until you understand yourself.

To enable you to better understand how your characteristics, interests, and needs can help you choose the most suitable job, we've prepared two informal inventories—Personality Profile and Working Conditions Inventory (see pages 3 and 4). If you spend some time with these inventories they will definitely help you to pinpoint your career direction.

Adjectives Describe You

To help you evaluate some of your personality traits, we have prepared a short list of adjectives. Simply circle those qualities that seem best to describe you. It is interesting to ask a friend or relative to choose the characteristics that he or she thinks best represent you. Analyze both sets of responses. You may be surprised to see the difference between how you perceive yourself and how others do.

When you have completed the checklist, analyze your responses in relationship to the descriptions of personality traits that are found in various fields.

independent	curious	easy-going
agreeable	sensitive	self-possessed
adaptable	tactful	quiet
abrupt	attractive	reserved
accommodating	poised	conservative

accepting	polished	chance-taker
administrative	forceful	gentle
altruistic	literate	follower
argumentive	energetic	leader
unassuming	shy	patient
businesslike	forceful	loner
relaxed	aggressive	orderly
professional	reliable	diplomatic
uncooperative	quick-tempered	flippant
dedicated	avid reader	do-gooder
fashion-minded	money-oriented	realistic
resourceful	bookish	humane
tenacious	high-energy	sensitive
extrovert	introvert	perfectionist
discreet	helpful	insightful
well-dressed	ambitious	moody
polished	important	cheerful
bad-tempered	confident	fast-thinking
competitive	sympathetic	fast-talking
informal	empathetic	happy
artistic	serious	kind
discreet	disciplined	bored
creative	good listener	hostile
honest	literary	irritable
unpleasant	lazy	

If you have personality traits that fall into the grouping of easy-going, tactful, serious, reliable, or business-like, you will fit into almost any field or industry. You will be an excellent candidate for a management trainee in a large Fortune 500 corporation as well as either a small or medium-sized company.

If along with those traits, you find that you checked off traits that cluster around such characteristics as ambitious, money-oriented, forceful, energetic, aggressive, high-energy, creative, competitive, confident, or self-possessed you'd be happy and successful in such fields as advertising, public relations, marketing, sales, publicity, or communications. Bear in mind that most large companies have their own marketing, advertising, and public relations departments so you're not limited to only agency positions. If you find the adjectives that best describe you cluster around such traits as kind, insightful, humane, sympathetic, tactful, conscientious, empathetic, good listener, helpful, and patient, it is very likely you'll find your niche in such fields as social services, personnel, or any area of the growing health fields.

Such traits as patience, orderliness, logical, perfectionist, curious, bashful, quiet, and serious, are among those that are shared by people successful in fields such as paralegal research, market research, libraries, education, copy editing, or specific areas of the computer industry.

Those who find their traits fall into groups such as well-dressed, extroverted, reliable, fashion-conscious, or polished should investigate jobs in the retailing, textile, or cosmetic industries.

Publishing (books, magazines, trade journals, and newspapers) is a good choice for those whose traits include literary, bookish, realistic, or tenacious. However, most college graduates are very naïve about the publishing field—they imagine it is an area of great creativity, dedicated to the search for great literature. Be aware that publishing is a business, and like any other business, its primary goal is to make a profit, often rejecting a very scholarly manuscript while paying a large advance for a work of lesser quality that they think might become a best seller. The recent graduate often makes a mistake in thinking of "editorial" as the only area in publishing that is career-oriented—there are also tremendous opportunities in book sales, publicity, subsidiary rights, and production.

As you probably note there are a number of what could be termed negative characteristics listed in this informal inventory. Although none of us is perfect and everyone has a periodic "bad" day, such traits as suspiciousness, impatience, and moodiness tend to work against you in both the getting of and being promoted in the job world. If you find you have checked more than five of these characteristics, you might discuss these feelings with a counselor.

Take a Personal Inventory

We've prepared a few questions which, if considered carefully, will give you more insights into your preferences and will help you in career evaluations. A space is provided for your answer to the right of the questions.

Your Deepest Feelings	Yes	No
1. I find I spend most of my leisure time in the evenings with friends rather than reading or pursuing some hobby or craft.		
2. I can be "turned on" by meeting new people and immediately feel comfortable.		
3. I can be "turned down" (take rejection) without being upset.		
4. I enjoy being in a competitive situation.		
5. I am a self-starter and like taking control over my destiny.		
6. In a group, I'm usually the person to initiate group activities.		
7. I am well motivated and I enjoy motivating other people.		
8. I like to take charge and persuade people to do things my way.		
9. I believe the pursuit of money is a realistic end in itself.		

Your Fundamental Philosophy	Yes	No
1. I'm the type of person who is happiest when being of service to others.		
2. I either have done, or would be interested in doing volunteer work with either physically or emotionally ill people.		

Your Fundamental Philosophy	**Yes**	**No**
3. People often come to me with their problems and I enjoy helping them to find solutions.		
4. I believe my work should somehow contribute to the betterment of society.		
5. I am comfortable with senior citizens as well as my own age group.		
6. I enjoy meeting new people.		
7. I can be with people with severe problems and still maintain my equilibrium and not become depressed.		
8. I feel that I have a lot of compassion.		
9. I'm the sort of person who needs to be needed.		
10. I'm responsive to other people and their needs.		

Your Preferred Working Conditions	**Yes**	**No**
1. I much prefer to spend a quiet evening reading, sewing, building models, or pursuing a hobby than being with a group of people.		
2. I feel I need a lot of privacy and enjoy being alone.		
3. I would rather work independently than as part of a team.		
4. I find I'm more productive when there is little or no pressure.		
5. I feel I work most effectively in a steady, even-paced environment.		
6. I like to know exactly what my work day will be like; in other words, I like to do the same things every day.		
7. Doing the same thing every day would bore me. I like a variety of challenges.		

Your Preferred Physical Surroundings	**Yes**	**No**
1. I am happiest in a restricted area, i.e., office, lab, classroom.		
2. I much prefer to work outdoors.		
3. I need to avoid places where people smoke.		
4. I like to work near home and not have a lengthy commute each day.		
5. I prefer the quiet time on the train, commuting to work.		
6. I must work where it is very quiet.		
7. I work better when there's lots going on around me.		

If most of you answer "yes" to most of the statements in the first list (Your Deepest Feelings) you will be very successful in those fields requiring leadership qualities and where there is a strong focus on financial gain. I suggest you slant your job campaign to the following industries:

Advertising
Business
Communications
Insurance
Finance (Investments, Banking)
Manufacturing
International Trade
Sales
Real Estate

If, on the other hand, you found that the statements in the second group were more "you," you would probably more likely find your needs in one of those organizations dedicated to a better world such as:

Social Science
Teaching
Rehabilitation
Health Fields
Social Service
Clergy, Rabbinate
Fund Raising
Foundations
Therapy and Counseling

The third set poses a very fundamental approach to how you perceive both pressure and variety. Pressure, to those who react badly to it, can produce a very unhealthy, stressful state. On the other hand, "one man's meat can be another man's poison," and to those who are stimulated by working against the odds, who thrive on pressure, can find working in a quiet, steady atmosphere cause for a rise in their blood pressure.

Those who answered "yes" to most of the statements in the third group will be happier in the nonpressure steady-paced working atmosphere. Generally, such jobs can be found in such fields as:

Libraries
Physical Sciences
Computer and Related Occupations
Insurance
Research
Banking

Conversely, those who answered "no" to the brief sentences in group 3 are motivated by pressure and should pursue careers in the following areas:

Business
Communications (Advertising, Publishing, Public Relations,
     Television)
Sales
Science Industries
Retailing

The physical surroundings you prefer actually break down to either an inside or an outside job, although other considerations such as convenience, ambiance, and comfort also come into play.

If you're happiest working "inside," you will find the majority of fields have definite space allocations. However, if you consider the atmosphere of the work place an important factor in your decision of which job to take, and you find the decor irritating, it is very likely that if you accept a job in that company, you will be uncomfortable and not be able to give that company your all.

For those of you opposed to working in a closed-in area, several fields offer possibilities:

Coaching (Athletics)
Archeology
Sales
Forestry
Landscape Architecture
Performing Arts
Law Enforcement

Where the Jobs Are

One of the biggest problems many liberal arts majors face is how to turn their academic knowledge into business skills. Very few openings are tailored for the graduating English major, whose college experiences have involved literary criticism and research. But these experiences have developed skills that can be applied successfully to certain fields. Advertising agencies, for example, may not be interested in the English major's knowledge of Chaucer, but they will like the way that major puts thoughts down on paper. Likewise, sociology majors may at graduation be intellectually involved in the development of early humankind, but that understanding of people and their motivations can be applied very nicely to market research or to the problems of personnel management at a large corporation.

The trick is knowing in which fields a major is most likely to apply best. The general intellectual development you have gained from your education can be applied to all types of work, but you will have an easier time getting that foot in the door if you head directly to certain industries or businesses. The following is a listing of suggested fields of work, matched to the college majors that are most popular today. Obviously, we have omitted business majors from this listing because there is a far more direct correlation with the business world.

ART MAJORS/ART HISTORY MAJORS.
Jobs consist of commercial art work, receptionists, selling art objects, and secretarial. Try:

• art departments of advertising agencies
• book production
• art galleries, fine graphic arts houses
• museums.

COMMUNICATIONS MAJOR/BROADCASTING/SPEECH.
Jobs can include production, script writing, film editing, collecting of props. Try:

- radio and television stations, radio and television packaging firms
- film producers
- departments within educational organizations.

ENGLISH MAJORS.
(also Journalism, English Literature, American Studies, Writing, Philosophy). Try:

- Publishing, including books, magazines (both trade and consumer), house organs, newspapers, etc.; also college travelers.
- Advertising, including copy departments of agencies, advertising departments of industry—writing brochures, catalogues, space ads, television scripts, continuity copy, promotional literature, direct mail, etc.
- Public Relations, agencies, public relations, non-profit organizations, fund raisers, press releases, feature articles, brochures, pamphlets, etc.
- Industry, management trainee, sales, economic, statistical, marketing.

GOVERNMENT/POLITICAL SCIENCE MAJORS.
The fortunate ones will be attending UN sessions, writing speeches, releases and features. There are a few openings on the various publications or organizations involved in international and national affairs. Also management and sales. Try:

- international affairs, history educational foundations
- diplomatic services, United Nations, embassies.

LANGUAGE MAJORS.
A few hard-to-get translation jobs in publishing. Try:

- international export, departments of banking, industry
- specialized schools, diplomatic services, United Nations, embassies, import-export firms.

MUSIC MAJOR.
Try:

- music publishers, record companies
- music departments of television in both studios and advertising agencies
- TV commercials.

MATH MAJORS.
Jobs generally consist of trainee positions working with statistics, analyses, computing, business trends, etc. Try:

- insurance, banking, investment companies, market research, media departments

- insurance, banking, investment companies, market research, media departments
- advertising agencies, programming, management consultants
- research for industry and nonprofit departments.

PSYCHOLOGY, SOCIOLOGY, ANTHROPOLOGY MAJORS.

Job generally covers statistical analysis, questionnaire service covers case aides and recreation work. Youth work covers programming, recreation, and administration. Also management and sales. Try:

- market research, personnel
- market research department of advertising agencies, social work, youth work.

The Current Job Market

One day the stock market is up, the next day it is down. Is the recession over? Is it beginning again? Is the economy really getting better? Everything (the gross national product, interest rates, employment figures) seems to indicate that the recession has hit bottom and we are going into a period of better economic conditions. This will mean an increase in hiring, more job openings, and less trauma in finding the perfect job for you.

However, you must realize that whether the economy is booming or sluggish, there are always job openings. Companies are forever recruiting. Some employees are promoted, others are transferred or retired, and, in consquence, staff vacancies are created and someone must be hired to fill them. Budget-minded companies often hire recent "trainable" college graduates at less money than experienced people who will demand higher salaries.

According to the U.S. Department of Labor, Division of Occupational Outlook, job prospects are good. Employment is expected to increase throughout the 1980s, provided that past trends continue, there is no war (in which case, there will be more jobs available), that unemployment does not exceed a specific level, and that our system of government and basic social levels do not change.

How to Get Information

The U.S. Department of Labor offers many publications extremely useful to the job seeker. I would recommend you glance through "The U.S. Department of Labor Statistics," which surveys every job category discussing educational requirements, the employment outlook, and the salary ranges being offered.

"The Job Outlook in Brief" in the *Occupational Outlook Quarterly* lists those jobs that will show the fastest growth. U.S. Department of Labor reports some very interesting facts to the job seeker. It's worthwhile to spend some time studying it and try to use the information to your advantage.

On page 10 are two tables which show fields that have the greatest opportunity at the present time. Table 1 lists the fastest-growing jobs, with the projected number of openings until 1990. Table 2 shows those jobs with the highest number of openings through to 1990. Consider both of these groupings when you are looking for a general field or considering a specific job.

TABLE 1   TABLE 2

Fastest-growing Jobs, 1978-90		Jobs With the Most Openings, 1978-90	
Occupation	Annual openings	Occupation	Annual openings
Bank Clerks	45,000	Secretaries and stenographers	305,000
Bank officers and financial managers	28,000	Retail sales workers	226,000
Business machine repairers	4,200	Building custodians	180,000
City managers	350	Cashiers	119,000
Computer service technicians	5,400	Bookkeeping workers	96,000
Construction inspectors	2,200	Nursing aides, orderlies, and attendants	94,000
Dental assistants	11,000	Cooks and chefs	86,000
Dental hygienists	6,000	Kindergarten and elementary teachers	86,000
Dining room attendants and dishwashers	37,000	Registered nurses	85,000
Flight attendants	4,800	Assemblers	77,000
Guards	70,000	Waiters and waitresses	70,000
Health service administrators	18,000	Guards	70,000
Homemaker-home health aides	36,000	Blue-collar worker supervisors	69,000
Industrial machinery repairers	58,000	Local truck drivers	64,000
Landscape architects	1,100	Accountants	61,000
Licensed practical nurses	60,000	Licensed practical nurses	60,000
Lithographers	2,300	Typists	59,000
Nursing aides, orderlies, and attendants	94,000	Carpenters	58,000
Occupational therapists	2,500	Industrial machinery repairers	58,000
Occupational therapy assistants	1,100	Real estate agents and brokers	50,000
Physical therapists	2,700	Construction laborers	49,000
Podiatrists	600	Engineers	46,500
Respiratory therapy workers	5,000	Bank clerks	45,000
Speech pathologists and audiologists	3,900	Private household workers	45,000
Teacher aides	26,000	Receptionists	41,000
Travel agents	1,900	Wholesale trade sales workers	40,000

Note: For these occupations, employment in 1990 is projected to be at least 50 percent higher than it was in 1978.

Note: Replacement needs and growth are projected to cause these occupations to offer the largest numbers of openings. Competition for openings will vary by occupation.

Source: Occupational Outlook Quarterly, U.S. Department of Labor

On page 11 you will find a chart published in the *Occupational Outlook Quarterly*, showing the average 1981 weekly salaries (before tax deductions) in a variety of fields. These figures include overtime, commissions, or tips. They relate *only* to earnings from salaries or wages, and not to those people who are self-employed. Usually, the earning power of the self-employed is higher in any occupation than that of the salaried worker. That is why physicians, who are generally self-employed and enjoy the highest income of all the occupations, are listed in the fourteenth position. That figure, $505, is the average of only those doctors who work for someone else.

These figures represent average earnings—that is, the salaries of the new graduates are included in the wages of the highly experienced—therefore, the earnings of each occupation may seem low. Remember, too, the span of income in a single occupation can be very broad.

It is interesting to note that occupations that require the highest level of education offer the highest salaries: engineers, lawyers, computer systems analysts. Study the top twenty and think about whether you should continue your education (at night, weekends, or through colleges offering home-study courses) to qualify you for a career in one of the higher-paying fields.

Weekly Earnings by Occupation

Rank/title	weekly pay	No. Job in field
1. Engineers, aeronautical	$614	82,000
2. Engineers, chemical	575	65,000
3. Engineers, electrical	549	370,000
4. Lawyers	546	548,000
5. Engineers, mechanical	540	247,000
6. Sales managers, except retail trade	540	367,000
7. Economists	536	157,000
8. Stock, bond sales agents	535	156,000
9. Engineers, industrial	530	231,000
10. Airplane pilots	530	80,000
11. Engineers, other	527	241,000
12. Computer systems analysts	519	209,000
13. Engineers, civil	505	183,000
14. Physicians—medical, osteopathic	501	436,000
15. School administrators, college	491	137,000
16. Operations, systems researchers	485	196,000
17. School administrators, elementary, secondary	475	289,000
18. Chemists	467	134,000
19. Authors	464	71,000
20. Pharmacists	463	147,000
21. Structural metal crafts workers	455	80,000
22. Millwrights	443	102,000
23. Officials, public administration	441	469,000
24. Sales representatives, manufacturing	434	410,000
25. Tool, diemakers	433	170,000
26. Health administrators	431	216,000
27. Other managers, administrators	431	6,504,000
28. Officials of lodges, unions	429	116,000
29. Architects	428	91,000
30. Aircraft mechanics	427	119,000
31. Biological scientists	423	57,000
32. Computer programmers	422	357,000
33. Designers	421	213,000
34. Electricians	419	639,000
35. College and university teachers	417	66,000
36. English teachers	416	53,000
37. Mine operatives	413	260,000
38. Health specialties teachers	412	52,000
39. Telephone installers, repairers	412	318,000
40. Bank officers, financial managers	411	680,000

Source: Occupational Outlook Quarterly

Your Résumé

Your number one assignment, and perhaps the most difficult task facing you in your job campaign, is the preparation of your résumé.

When you consider the average résumé reader spends no more than thirty seconds skimming each résumé, it becomes apparent that your résumé must *stand out*—it has to be superior to the others that represent your competition, it is imperative that it is easy to read, that the facts must be prominent and convincing, and that it incites enough interest in you to result in an interview.

Granted a résumé, no matter how cleverly written, can never reveal the many facets that make the total you—your talents, abilities, special skills, hopes, and aspirations. If your two-dimensional résumé cannot possibly duplicate the three-dimensional you, then exactly what is its purpose? In this complex, sophisticated world where time, distance, and sheer numbers of individuals work against personal involvement between every employee and employer, the résumé has been adopted as a facsimile of you. Because it must represent you and interest the potential employer enough to want to see you, it has become very important—indeed, it is a vital document.

Think of your résumé as your personal dossier, your proxy, your statement of self—in other words, that which represents you. You must keep in mind that your résumé will be seen by many people involved in the hiring process, and each will examine it, judge it, and decide on this basis whether to invite you for an interview or whether it is a candidate, like so many others, to be simply discarded.

It is also helpful to think of your résumé as an advertisement—an advertisment whose product is *you!* We all recognize an ad that sells: it is brief, it contains strong facts, and those facts are prominent, convincing, and easy to read.

Writing your résumé will take time and much thought but once you are aware of the logic involved in its preparation, I can guarantee that you'll not only have the ability to write a job-getting résumé, but you'll find a great deal of satisfaction in acquiring a new skill.

How Long Should a Résumé Be?

Résumés come in all sizes (we've received just as many on scraps of paper, 3″ × 5″ cards, as ten- to fifteen-page autobiographies), yet there is just one *correct* size—regular 8½″ × 11″. It is easily filed, easily handled, and adds a professional touch.

A recent college graduate hasn't yet had enough experiences to warrant more than one page. Anything longer is a tip-off that you are unable to make a judgment on the difference between the important facts and what might be considered unnecessary information.

It is the function of the résumé to describe and identify its writer in the most positive manner. Though every résumé—like every individual—is different, all must contain the following information:

1. Your name, address, and phone number. If you're sending out résumés while still in college, it is wise to give the phone number where you can be reached after you have graduated. In your cover letter, be sure to mention when you will be available for interviews.
2. Educational History. Name and Address of College and which degree received. (If you maintained an average of 3.0 out of a baseline of 4.0, that's something to be proud of—be sure that it is mentioned in your résumé. On the other hand, if you barely graduated or maintained a consistently low average, don't include it in your résumé. Very likely it will be brought up in an interview, and we'll discuss how to handle it in Chapter 8.)
3. Any honor you were awarded. Membership in scholarly organizations. If you were Phi Beta Kappa, be proud of it. Be sure it is on your résumé.
4. Brief descriptions of work history. Example: summer jobs as part-time employment, internships, co-op education programs.
5. List any languages in which you are fluent.
6. List any skills you have, such as, typing, word processing, etc. You may or may not include (in other words, optional) personal data such as age, height, weight, marital status; job objective or career goal; military or draft status; willingness to travel or relocate; or information about your hobbies.

You must never insert the following in your résumé:

1. Salary expectations
2. Salaries of summer jobs
3. Name of husband or wife
4. Name and addresses of references
5. Photograph

Though there are several accepted styles of résumés (Historical or Chronical, Functional, Analytical, Synopsis/Amplified), the style appropriate for most recent graduates is the one that lists the facts in a historical/chronological manner.

Historical or Chronological

As the name implies, this style of résumé presents the information in chronological succession. It is necessary, however, that the presentation be in *inverse* chronological order, starting with your present educational experience and moving backwards, listing your most recent summer experiences first.

Dates are always included. They can be displayed in a vertical column set apart from the other information or included as an intergral part of each paragraph of your history. Generally, the first is preferred, as mostemployers like to be able to determine at a glance the dates involved.

If you decide to include a job objective, it would be placed at the very beginning, after your name and address but before the descriptions of your education and work history.

Job Objective or Career Goal

Deciding to use a Job Objective or Career Goal (the two mean very much the same thing) will depend on whether its use will actually increase the power of your résumé.

Remember, the use of the Career Goal is up to you — it's completely optional. If you do decide to use the Job Objective, it should be brief—no more than two sentences. In one or two lines it should be a statement that briefly summarizes your goals and is justified by your education.

You should avoid stating an objective that is too limiting. I remember one graduate who most wanted a job in children's book publishing. She would, however, have been very happy to accept *any* job in publishing, whether it be trade books, textbooks, magazines, or trade journals. She sent her résumé to every publisher listed in the Yellow Pages but, unfortunately, she didn't get any bites. It is quite obvious that if a textbook publisher received her résumé and had an opening, he or she would *not* have considered her because she specified a job in children's book publishing. Obviously, her Career Objective was *too specific*. A more appropriate goal would have been "To secure an entry-level position in publishing." She might have been even wiser to not include any job objective.

Be careful to avoid the use of clichés—"A challenging job where I can meet people," "A position that is both responsible and creative." Such career goals don't really say anything, and your résumé would be more professional if such a statement were not included.

If you can transfer your education, talents, or skills into a position or specific job title, that makes for an ideal "Job Objective." For example:

> Chemist
> Laboratory Assistant
> Staff Accountant
> Salesperson Trainee
> Gal/Guy Friday

Another approach is to use a field as the Job Objective: For example:

> An entry-level position in any areas of Advertising
> Growth spot in major corporation

Your Career Goal doesn't have to be limited to either a job title or a field. It may simply be a statement of what or in which direction you hope to be going. Don't include the pronoun "I" or "me." Be sure the goal is brief, assertive, and to the point. For example:

> To utilize mathematics background in the computer industry

A sales position which might ultimately lead to a career in marketing

An entry-level position in journalism

If you plan to use your résumé in a mass mailing and also to use it to respond to a large number of classified advertisements, it may be a good idea to omit the Career Goal and include it in the covering letter. This allows you to target your goal to the specific situation.

Educational History

As a recent college graduate, the most valuable asset you have to sell is your education, and, therefore, it is placed at the very beginning of your résumé unless you have decided to state a Career Goal. If you use a Job Objective, your educational history should immediately follow that statement. If you are not including a Job Objective, your educational history should be placed directly under your name, address, and phone number.

Your education should be arranged in reverse chronological order. Begin with your most advanced or recent degree, and work backwards until you reach your bachelor's degree. Obviously, if you don't have an advanced degree, start with your bachelor's degree. It is not necessary for a college graduate to list a high school unless the secondary education was a very prestigious preparatory school and naming it might enhance the résumé.

Be sure to include the name and address (just the city, street address is not necessary) of your college or university, the date of graduation, and the degree you received. You should include your major and minor, as well as any honors that were earned. For example:

Advanced degree
Columbia University
New York, NY
1982 - PhD Political Science

College of William and Mary
Williamsburg, VA
1970 - M.S. International Affairs

College of New Rochelle
New Rochelle, NY
1968 - B.A. Magna Cum Laude
Major: Liberal Arts

No advanced degree
University of Chicago
Chicago, IL
1983 - B.A. Phi Beta Kappa 4.0 Average
Business Administration/Economics

Keep these tips in mind:

1. It is proper to abbreviate the title of your degree; that is, BS instead of Bachelor of Science.
2. List all honors, including languages, scholarships, and awards.
3. You can indicate your major and minor by using the words "Major" (followed by subject) and "Minor" (followed by subject), or simply use a slash. For example, "Major: Chemistry Minor: Biology" or simply "Chemistry/Biology."
4. If you attended more than one college or university, be sure to list all of them, again, in reverse chronological order. Don't forget to include dates but do omit any explanation of why you changed. This can be discussed in the interview. For example:

    1981 – 1983 BA University of Colorado, Denver, CO

    1979 – 1981 New York University, New York, NY

Work History

Even though your work history probably consists of summer and temporary jobs, it will add significant power to your résumé.

Your experience will contribute to the feeling of your being a mature, functioning adult or will—as one of our favorite clients used to say—let people know you are "office broken." Though you're looking for an entry-level position, you're not an "absolute beginner."

If you have worked on a job that relates to the career you desire, that would be ideal, but also highly unlikely. Students are expected to take any kind of job that they can get, and the fact that you could take a boring job and stick with it for a summer says a lot about your character and will be an asset on your résumé.

Your work background should immediately follow your educational history. Though you probably have only summer or temporary jobs, each should be listed separately. Each entry should include the name and address of the employer, the dates involved, the job title, and a brief description of your responsibilities. The description should be succinct, but should still include all basic activities of each particular job. Use implied pronouns; clear, simple language; and active verbs. Don't write in the third person (it is stylistically objectionable) and don't use "I" ("I" is redundant—the person reading the résumé knows you are the subject of your own résumé). For example, don't write "He or she was responsible for bookkeeping," or, "I was responsible for bookkeeping," but rather, "was responsible for bookkeeping."

If you worked while in college, that should be the first job listed, and the others should follow in reverse chronological order.

If you worked through a temporary agency and were sent to several different companies, give the name and address of the temporary service, the dates you were employed, your job title, and the names of the companies you were assigned to. For example:

Part Time	Library Assistant
1979–1983	Low Library, Columbia University, NY, NY Catalogued books, maintained library files and revised when necessary. Handled routine requests for materials, slides, and films. Ordered books, pamphlets, magazines as needed to keep library collection up to date.
Summer:	Gal/Guy Friday
1980, 1981, 1982	Career Blazers Temporary Personnel, Inc., New York, NY As Gal/Guy Friday was responsible for typing and editing correspondence, manuscripts, reports, press releases. Functioned as receptionist, set up appointments, and assumed general office duties.

The following is a few of the very many action verbs you might want to use:

Established	Initiated
Responsible for	Researched
Created	Motivated
In charge	Administrate
Supervise	Functioned
Originated	Direct
Organized	Contributed
Coordinate	Assist

Also remember that it is not necessary to use full sentences. The snappier simple phrases will be more effective.

Other Details

Extracurricular activities can be very important. Include a description of your extracurricular activities. It not only paints a more rounded portrait of you, but also indicates talents and abilities not reflected in your course of study.

Membership in the college debating society implies an articulate, poised personality. A class officer will be seen as an extroverted individual with a great deal of leadership potential. Being active in sports, such as football, basketball or tennis, indicates an individual who functions well on a team. If you have aspirations in communications, working on any college publications will give you an advantage.

These activities should be listed simply with no further explanation.

Editor of college yearbook
Photographer for college newspaper
Member of college debating society
President of chess club

Personal Information

There was a time, before the Civil Rights movement, when every résumé was expected to include height, weight, age, sex, and marital status. This is no longer necessary, optional at best. I really can't see any reason to include such information. I don't think any of the above is pertinent, nor will it strengthen your résumé.

If you are free to travel or to relocate, mention that in your résumé. Such information is solid, and would be very useful to a person screening résumés for a position out of town or requiring travel.

If you have traveled extensively, that might be of interest to certain employers and it should be noted in your résumé. The fact that your résumé shows you have been to the Far East may be the very thing that sparks the necessary interest in you to warrant an interview. Though we recommend that you include extensive travel in your résumé, we also want to remind you to keep it brief—no more than a sentence or two.

Skills

College graduates often make the mistake of not listing any skills they have acquired. They feel that holding a degree makes it unnecessary to mention they might be an excellent typist or have had experience in word processing, copy editing, typesetting, bookkeeping, or any one of the many office machines. They are selling themselves short. Any skill increases one's marketability. If you have them, flaunt them! I have had the experience of sending résumés of three college grads to a prestigious international foundation who was looking for a library/stock research assistant. Though the job specifications *did not* require typing, the client/employer chose to interview and hire the one person whose résumé indicated he could type. Their feeling was, it's always a good idea to have someone who might be able to pitch in if necessary. The other candidates, too, could type, but because it didn't show up on their résumés, they simply lost out.

Any knowledge of foreign languages should be noted in this section. Be sure to distinguish whether you are fluent in the language or have just a reading knowledge of it.

References

At the very end of your résumé, simply state "References available upon request."

The names of your references should never be included in your résumé. Not only is it unprofessional, but it can cause unnecessary bother to those persons listed. You should only give permission to call your references when an employer has indicated that he or she is really interested in employing you.

Always, of course, get permission from all the people you list as a reference before giving out their names. Try to choose people who can be reached quickly. It is preferable to list people who can be reached by phone rather than by mail. If you are giving the business phone of a reference, be certain that he or she is still employed by that company. If you have given a woman as a reference who has since married, make sure you know whether she is using her maiden or married name.

Likewise, if your name has changed through marriage or any other reason, be sure that your references know you by your new name. It is a good idea for a married woman to indicate both her married and maiden name.

If all your references are from college and you'll be job hunting in another city, it is a good idea to ask your references to write a paragraph or two about you to be left with the university placement officer. The placement office will keep these references on file and will send them on request (some placement offices charge a small fee for this service). This is a very efficient method and is helpful in minimizing the bother to those people cooperative enough to be used as a reference. If you are using this method, be sure to indicate on your résumé that your references are available through the college placement officer. Make sure each of your references has a copy of your résumé. It is courteous and will also help him or her to have the facts fresh in their minds.

Honesty is the Best Policy

No matter what the circumstance, the cardinal rule in writing your résumé is absolute *honesty*. Include *nothing* in your résumé that isn't completely true. The truth has a way of coming out and, once caught in a lie, you will have lost your credibility, which can be fatal. Such a loss cannot be corrected and will seriously damage your reputation. It puts an additional strain on you every time you interact with someone who has read your résumé. Be proud of what you have *accomplished*. You have earned your degree and have learned to accept your weaknesses as well as your strengths. You will get a job, I promise you, on your own merits and you won't always be in fear that you'll be "found out."

Before you can actually sit down and write your résumé, you must collect all the facts. The following worksheets will help you include all the necessary information and arrange it in a concise, organized manner. The worksheets are arranged in reverse chronological order; therefore, if you keep this factual information on the same form when actually writing the résumé, you will produce a résumé that will contain all the necessary information arranged correctly.

Take time to fill out the worksheets on pages 28–32 *carefully* as possible. Be sure all information is correct (it's a good idea to re-check the dates) because this information will become the heart and soul of your résumé.

You will find some sample layouts on pages 22–26, which will prove to be helpful.

Résumé Appeal

Since your résumé is the first contact between you, a whole network of people, and your prospective employer, it is imperative that it invites reading. The physical appearance of your résumé is as important as the information it contains. Logically, no matter how good the facts included in your résumé, if the résumé is hard to read or confusing to interpret, it will end up in the wastebasket. As a result, your superior qualifications will never be read and, therefore, never be considered. Be aware that your résumé is always competing with many others, and as a result it is scanned very rapidly. (Our inquiries have shown that "résumé readers" rarely give more than thirty seconds of attention to a résumé to decide if it merits a more detailed reading.) In other words, your résumé has thirty seconds to be chosen for the group to be considered. Obviously, the more attractive your résumé is, the better impression it will make in the few initial moments.

Name   Phone #

Street Address

City, State, Zipcode

Career Objective_____

Name of College_____ Date (from - to)

Address of College_____

Major/Minor

Degree

Class Standing

Awards, Honors, Scholarships

Job Title - Name of Company   Summer of _____
            Address of Company
Description of duties and responsibilities in this job.

Job Title - Name of Company   Summer of _____
            Address of Company
Description of responsibilities and duties in this job.

Job Title - Name of Company   Summer of _____
            Address of Company
Description of nature of employment, with duties and responsibilities.

Languages

Skills

Willing to Relocate

References (on request)

Name

Street Address

City, State, Zipcode

Home Phone #

Education: Name of College, Address of College (City, State)

from_____to_____ Degree: Major: Minor:

Experience:

from_____to_____ Job Title

                        Name of Company

Responsibilities_____

_____

from_____to_____ Job Title

                        Name of Company

                        Address of Company

Responsibilities_____

_____

from_____to_____ Job Title

                        Name of Company

                        Address of Company

Responsibilities_____

_____

Honors:

Awards:

Skills:

References: Available on request

Resume of:

Name

Street Address   Home Phone #
City, State, Zipcode

Career Objective: (optional)

Educational History

                                  Degree - Name of College
from (date)   Address of College
to   (date)   Average (only use if
                                                   3.0 or more
                                                   out of 4.0)
                                          Major/Minor

Honors/Awards   _____

Employment History
from (date)   Job Title Name of Company
to   (date)   Address of Company
                                  Brief description of job duties
                                  and responsibilities.

from (date)   Job Title Name of Company
to   (date)   Address of Company
                                  Brief description of job duties
                                  and responsibilities.

from (date)   Job Title Name of Company
to   (date)   Address of Company
                                  Brief description of job duties
                                  and responsibilities.

Languages   _____

Skills   _____

References   Furnished on request

Name
Street Address
City, State, Zipcode
Home Phone #

Education

From (date)   Name of College
To (date)   Address of College
     Advanced Degree   Major   Minor
     GPA (include only if it is above
         3.0 out of a possible 4.0)

From (date)   Name of College
To (date)   Address of College
     Degree
     GPA (include only if it presents
         your academic record favorably)

Honors/Awards

Date received   _____

Date received   _____

Employment History (placed in reverse chronological order)

From (date)   <u>Your Job Title</u>
To (date) or   Employer, Address
summer of _____   Job duties (2 to 4 lines)

From (date)   <u>Your Job Title</u>
To (date)   Employer, Address
     Job duties (2 to 4 lines)

From (date)   <u>Your Job Title</u>
To (date)   Employer, Address
     Job duties (2 to 4 lines)

Extracurricular Activities

_____

_____

Language Fluency

_____

_____

Skills

_____

References

     Furnished on request

Name   Home Phone #
Street Address
City, State, Zipcode

CAREER OBJECTIVE (optional)

EDUCATIONAL HISTORY

Name of College   From (date)
Address of College   To   (date)
Advanced Degree
GPA (include only if it is 3.0, or above, out of a possible 4.0)

Name of College   From (date)
Address of College   To   (date)
Bachelor's Degree — Major/Minor
GPA (optional)

HONORS AND AWARDS

_____   Dates Received

_____

EXTRACURRICULAR ACTIVITIES

_____

_____

EMPLOYMENT HISTORY (summer jobs)

JOB TITLE
Name of Company   From (date)
Address of Company   To   (date)

(Description of duties and responsibilities in above company — 2 to 4 lines)

JOB TITLE
Name of Company   From (date)
Address of Company   To   (date)
Description of duties and responsibilities.

JOB TITLE
Name of Company   From (date)
Address of Company   To   (date)
Description of duties and responsibilities.

LANGUAGE FLUENCY

SKILLS

REFERENCES
Available on Request

Drafting Your Own Résumé

Note that these drafts are to be considered solely as models. You may wish to make deviations in your own résumé. We've included 2 worksheets, one for practice and one for your final version.

When you have filled out the worksheets, you will be well on your way to writing your résumé. The information included in the worksheets comprises the very "guts" of your résumé. For that reason you must thoroughly check what you have written to make absolutely sure everything is correct.

1. Look at the dates. Are they correct?
2. *Reread* your résumé worksheets. Is there any important information missing?
3. Examine the worksheets. Have you included any information that is not necessary? (Such as name of husband or wife; list of all the courses you took; name of grammar school; your salary minimum, or salaries of past jobs.)
4. Reread *each* of your "Job Duties." Are they as brief as possible? Are they written in the most positive manner possible? Have you used as many action verbs as you could? Have you *excluded* all pronouns?
6. If you listed any scholarships, will the average reader understand the nature of the scholarship?
7. Reread your worksheets *again* to make sure there are no words spelled incorrectly. Ask at least two people to proofread your worksheets, concentrating on the spelling. If in doubt, refer to your dictionary.

Worksheet for Entry-Level College Graduate

I. Name:

_____

(If married woman, include married and maiden name)

Address: _____

_____

_____

(Be sure to give home, not college, address. Give street and number, city, state, and zipcode)

Phone (home):_____

(Be sure to give area code)

Phone (other): _____

(If there is anybody else who can take messages—mother, father, business, or friend—be sure to list full name of person who will take messages. Don't forget the area code and if that person has an extension, be sure to include it.)

II. Job Objective or Career Goal:

Remember, the Job Objective is optional. If you decide to use it, be brief and careful that your stated objective *does not* limit your opportunities nor is so vague as to be meaningless.

_____

_____

_____

_____

III. Educational Background

Begin with your most advanced degree and, in REVERSE CHRONOLOGICAL ORDER, list all degrees and certificates stopping with your bachelor's degree. Be sure to list the name and address (just city and state) along with dates of attendance.

Dates: Name of University or College:

____   ____   _____

(From)   (To)   (or the date degree received)

_____

                    Address of School: _____

                    _____

                    (City and State) _____

                    _____

                    Degree Earned: (or credits earned)

                    _____

Major: _____   Minor: _____

(If PhD, title of your thesis instead of minor)

Dates: Name of School
____   ____   _____
(From) (To)   (or the date degree received)

Address of School: _____

_____

(City and State) _____

_____

Degree Earned: (or credits earned)

_____

Major: _____   Minor: _____

Dates: Name of School:
____   ____   _____
(From) (To)   (or the date degree received)

Address of School: _____

_____

(City and State) _____

_____

Degree Earned:

_____

Major: _____   Minor: _____

If you changed colleges, be sure to list both and treat dates from year to year.

Scholarships, honors, awards including dates

Scholarships:

_____

Awards:

_____

Honors:

_____

Class Standing or Grade Average (list only if noteworthy)

_____

IV. Employment History (summer or part-time jobs)
Your employment history should be listed in reverse chronological order.
(Starting with your most recent job first. If you worked *part-time* while in
college as well as during summers, you should list the job you held while
in college first.)

Dates: Name of Company:

____   ____   _____

From   To
mo/yr   mo/yr
           Address of Company:

           _____

           (No street address; simply city and state)

           Job Title:

           _____

           Description of Responsibilities:
           (Remember, keep it brief; use action verbs)

           _____

           _____

           _____

           _____

Dates: Name of Company:

____   ____   _____

           Address of Company:

           _____

           Job Title:

           _____

           Description of Responsibilities: _____

           _____

           _____

Dates: Name of Company:

____   ____   _____

From   To
mo/yr   mo/yr   Address of Company:

           _____

           Job Title:

           _____

Description of Responsibilities: _____

_____

_____

Dates: Name of Company:

_____

From   To
mo/yr   mo/yr   Address of Company:

_____

Job Title:

_____

Description of Responsibilities: _____

_____

V. List Extracurricular Activities: Class Officer, Membership in School Organizations:

_____

_____

_____

VI. Other Skills and Abilities:

Languages (indicate degree of fluency—reading, speaking or writing):

_____

Office Machines:

_____

_____

_____

VII. Special Interests or Hobbies: (Remember, this is optional)

_____

VIII. References:

Though the names, addresses and phone number of your references should never be included in your résumé, it is a good idea to assemble all necessary data at the same time you are preparing your résumé. That will help keep you organized. Try to have a minimum of three people as references.

Remember, though, we're getting this information together; IT WILL NOT APPEAR ON YOUR RÉSUMÉ.

Note: Give complete address—street and number, city, state, and zipcode. Give area code with telephone numbers. (Give business address and telephone number instead of home information. It is much more professional and, obviously, if your reference is not employed, give home address and phone describing your relationship to him or her.)

Name of Reference: _____

Position: _____

Company Affiliation: _____

Company Address: _____

_____

Business Phone and Extension: _____

Name of Reference: _____

Position: _____

Company Affiliation: _____

Company Address: _____

_____

Business Phone and Extension: _____

Name of Reference: _____

Company Affiliation: _____

Company Address: _____

_____

Business Phone and Extension: _____

Name of Reference: _____

Position: _____

Company Affiliation: _____

Company Address: _____

Business Phone and Extension: _____

If reference is not employed:
Name of Reference: _____

Relationship to you: _____
ie. Teacher, Professor, Member of the Clergy

Address of Reference: _____

_____

Home Phone Number: _____

On pages 38-117 you will see a great number of sample résumés in addition to the sample layouts on pages 22–26. One of them, or a combination of several, may appeal to you as a format you might like to follow. Sketch out the form you decide to use and, with your completed worksheets, you are ready to start writing.

Don't be discouraged if the first few drafts are not completely satisfying. I am sure you have had the experience of rewriting term papers several times before handing them in. Though I have mentioned it before, I again must stress that your résumé is such a vital part of your job campaign that every hour spent on it will ultimately pay off.

Keep in mind that your résumé will determine whether or not an employer will want to meet you. Certainly, if you are not interviewed by a certain company, you will have absolutely no chance of getting hired. If you think of your résumé as a passport to a good job — a document that can literally determine your future — you won't resent the time involved in preparing the very best résumé.

After you have completed a résumé that meets with your satisfaction, I suggest you give yourself a break and then reread it the following day. For some reason (although you are not consciously thinking about it) the subconscious continues to mull over your problem. The next day, the task which yesterday seemed Herculean in magnitude becomes a very uncomplicated, extremely solvable challenge.

This is a good thing to remember and use to your advantage. Whenever you have a problem which seems overwhelming, let go. Sleep on it, and I'll bet anything that by the next day you will come up with so many solutions that it will be hard for you to remember how just yesterday that problem seemed unsolvable. Forgetting philosophy and getting back to the résumés—

The next thing you have to consider before typing the résumé is the layout of the copy. You might choose the format from one of our sample résumés or sample layouts. You might decide to combine two or more samples, or start from scratch and create your own. Whatever layout you decide upon, make sure that the total effect is pleasing to the eye, easy to read, and the different sections (identification information, educational history, work experiences, etc.) are clearly separated from one another.

We've received literally thousands of résumés at the agency and have come across every conceivable size, shape, and color. For just about three seconds they have attracted our staff's attention—and then they are quickly discarded. Résumés made to look like restaurant menus, newspapers with the headline "John Doe (or whoever) is Ready to Work," Valentines, brochures, invitations, summonses, subpoenas, licenses, diplomas, checks, money orders, telegrams, mailgrams, etc., are immediately discarded. Not only are we aware that our clients would have zero interest in these "imaginative(?)" novellas but they are simply too cumbersome to file.

Use standard 8½" x 11" paper; not only is this size easiest to handle and to file, but it is the most professional.

Choose a good-quality bond paper and use only one side of the paper. Usually one uses white, but you may choose a pale color as long as it will contrast well with the type. Make sure the typeface you choose is neat and easy to read. It should not be so large that it overwhelms the space it is in. It should be conservative and not too "arty."

Use your ground—the white space on the paper—effectively, even using your margins imaginatively. Use at least half-inch margins on all four sides. White space is soothing to the eye, and you should plan to interrupt your copy with enough white space to allow the reader to rest her or his eyes while reading your résumé.

Your typewriter, used with imagination and good taste, can be very helpful in creating an attractive résumé. You might use upper and lower case in combination with all caps, or if you have an IBM Selectric typewriter, mix various types. Create borders; use dots and dashes and asterisks for emphasis or separating sections.

If you are not really an *excellent* typist, it is a good idea to have a professional do it for you. Actually, whatever it costs is a small expense considering the ultimate return that a superior résumé can bring to you. Be absolutely sure that there are no typing or spelling errors—proofread, proofread, and then have a friend proofread. If you have used a typing or professional service, don't accept or pay for the résumés until they are thoroughly checked for accuracy. Certain résumés are discarded immediately even though the contents may be completely on target. Why? Simply because they are not dressed well. They look sloppy. They allow the reader to infer a negative image of its writer. Some of the unpleasant images of the writer conjured by faulty résumés include:

no planned format (uneven margins, no spaces between categories, etc.)	underqualified
	typographical errors
	sloppy
disorganized	grammatical errors
misspelled words	incompetent

At one time employers expected every résumé they received to be typed individually. Fortunately, those days have passed. Although carbon copies (because of smudging and lack of clarity) are not acceptable, any other duplicating process which turns out clean, sharp copies may be used.

Photocopying, offset printing, and multilith processing all give excellent results. Xerox copies are admissible as long as they are sharp, clear, and easy to read. It is obvious that if you are willing to spend the money on having your résumé printed, the results will surely be good looking as well as very professional.

As the success of your campaign may very likely hinge upon the appearance of your résumé, it is imperative you choose a service that turns out a professional-looking product. These services are listed in the Yellow Pages under Copy and Duplicating Services, Offset Reproductions, and Typing Services.

It is important that your résumé be reproduced on good-quality paper. If you are having typescript reproduced, be sure to insist on good-quality bond paper. If it is printed from hot or cold type, an equally fine opaque paper should be used. Don't skimp on the cost of paper. The extra expense is minimal, and the effect it creates is well worth it. It doesn't pay to order a small number either, because the cost doesn't increase that much with the additional quantity printed. It is not unrealistic for a recent graduate to arm him/or hreself with one hundred résumés.

Sample Résumés

The résumés reproduced in this chapter have been categorized as follows:

General
Business
Specialized Fields

This categorization should help you isolate those résumés that come closest to what yours will eventually be like. The first—General—includes all majors from the liberal arts and sciences. These are résumés from recent graduates who have very little work experience and for whom the educational information is strongest. Examine the samples and notice how each attempts to display the candidate's strengths and to apply general educational skills to a business or industry. Some résumés are multipurpose, and could be sent to one of many types of businesses; others are more specific, targeted toward a particular objective.

The second grouping—Business—is a sampling of résumés from students who have majored in an area of business. For these candidates, the connection with business is easier to make, and the objective in the résumé is to show particular strengths in the field or to state goals within the industry.

The last category—Specialized Fields—encompasses résumés from graduates with special degrees or fields of interest. It is a catchall grouping, ranging from education majors to engineering. Candidates in these situations usually have enough material to make a solid résumé, but choosing the appropriate format and organizing the information can sometimes present problems.

If you have the time, skim all the samples in this chapter. It may well be that suggestions for several of your résumé entries will appear in résumés completely different from your own.

General

Dorothy Nelson
72 Roberts Street
Tulsa, Oklahoma 74105
(918) 621-4434

Education:

June, 1984   B.A., Anthropology
                              Tulsa State College, Tulsa, Okla.

Academic Honors: Dean's List 1984, 1983, 1982

Work History:

1982-1984   RESEARCH ASSISTANT
                              Museum of Natural History
                              Tulsa State College, Tulsa, Oklahoma
                              Served as secretary to Director of Museum.
                              Duties included typing, filing, general
                              office work. Set up meetings, conferences,
                              travel reservations. Checked new museum
                              displays.

Summer, 1981   CLERK
                              Honeywell Oil Company, Tulsa, Oklahoma
                              General typing, filing, reception duties;
                              responsible for collecting data in
                              preparation of computer programming.

Summer, 1981   TUTOR
                              Tulsa State College, Tulsa, Oklahoma
                              Tutored 25 students in all freshman subjects.

Extracurricular
Activities: President, American Anthropology Society, 1982,
                              83, 84

References: Available on request

Harold Flynn
6 Palisades Rd.
Yonkers, N.Y. 10703
(914) 968-2243

Education History

1984

B.A. Sociology
City College of New York, New York City

Employment History

1982-1984

Security Guard, Riverview Apartments
Monitor closed circuit television systems,
secure alarms systems, control tenant access,
run identification checks

1982-1983

Manager, 1085 Warburton Avenue
Liaison to the public telephone and counter
sales, checked customers using TSW credit systems,
collected rent, showed and rented apartments.
Maintained customer records, prepared invoices and
receipts, updated and maintained tenant files, light
bookkeeping and clerical records.

1981-1982

Secretary, Parker Real Estate, Yonkers, N.Y.
Typing, steno, filing, general office duties,
receptionist, greeted visitors, ran switchboard
555, sent out bills, checked receipts.

References

On request

MARSHA HENDERSON   35 Valley Road   Los Angeles, California 90012
                                     (213) 675-2157

Education
    B.A.   University of California at Los Angeles   1983
    Major: Sociology and Education   Minor: English

Experience
9/82-6/83   STUDENT TEACHER
               Hopewell Child Learning Center
               Santa Monica, California
               Responsible for teaching academic, social and swimming
               program to three- and four-year-old children.
               Administered tests. Conferred with parents and
               suggested special help when needed.

9/81-6/82   RECEPTIONIST (part-time)
               Caroline and Deane Advertising   Los Angeles
               Handled typing, correspondence, and phone calls for
               President and Vice-President in addition to extensive
               contact with clients.

References   Provided upon request.

David Gotz
58 North Street
Omaha, Nebraska 68114
(402) 456-7161

Career Objective
A challenging position in sociological/survey research and planning.

Education
University of Nebraska   Omaha, Nebraska
M.S., Natural Resources Planning   1983
B.S., Geology   1979

Professional Development
September 1982 - Present
UPDATE, INC.   Omaha, Nebraska
Involved in both market and leisure research for this private consulting firm. Primary responsibilities include background research data entry and analysis, SPSS and graphic programming, and letter writing.

September 1979 - September 1981
School of Natural Resources, University of Nebraska
Graduate research and teaching assistant involved in the design, administration, and analysis (SPSS, SCSS) of social surveys. Instructed courses in natural resource management theory.

Affiliations
Wilderness Society
National Wildlife Federation

References on Request

Marcia Peterson
2 Raleigh Street
Princeton, New Jersey 08540
(609) 636-2329

Education:
1980-1984   B.A. Art History
                                   Vassar College, Poughkeepsie, New York
Honors: G.P.A. 3.9
                                   Graduated Summa Cum Laude

Work Experience:
1982-1984   Curator's Assistant
                                   Vassar College, Poughkeepsie, N.Y.
                                   Assisted curator with collections, inventory,
                                   exhibitions, scheduling, displays, lecture
                                   programs and shows.
1982-1984   Secretary, Art History Department
                                   Vassar College, Poughkeepsie, N.Y.
                                   Assisted professor in preparation of lectures,
                                   slides, pictures, typing and correspondence.
Interests: Music, Swimming
Skills: Typing 60 wpm, Word processing (IBM)
References: On request

Laurie Abrams
34 Pollypark Road
Harrison, New York   10528   (914) 835-2661

Education
1979-1983   Brown University
                             B.A. Studio Art
                             Includes study at London School of Art, England
                             and Rhode Island School of Design

Employment
6/82-9/82   Design Plus Inc.
                             Yorktown Heights, NY
                             General boardwork

6/80-9/80   Miller Lithography, Inc.
                             Scarsdale, NY
                             Mechanicals and paste-ups

6/79-8/79   Camp Belvedere
                             Lee, MA
                             Art Instructor

Honors   First Prize, Art Contest City Bank, Harrison, NY
and Awards   Alumni Award Harrison High School
                             National Merit Scholarship

Activities   Art Student Group, counseling program
                             Brown University Swim Team

References   Available on request

RESUME OF
SUSAN LOPEZ

ADDRESS
10 Smythe Street
Peeksill, New York 11304
(914) 227-1567

EDUCATION
1979-1983: Rutgers University, B.A. Studio Art.

1970: Syracuse University, Photography and Art Workshop.

EMPLOYMENT
1983-Present: Paste-up artist, Design Technologies,
New Rochelle, N.Y.

1983-Summer: General boardwork, High Times Magazine,
New York, N.Y.

1981-Summer: Mechanical, paste-up artist,
Lasky Company Lithographers, Millburn, N.J.

1980-Summer: Art Instructor, Camp Rondack, N.Y.

HONORS AND
AWARDS
Salutatorian, Morristown High School.
First Prize, Art Contest, City Federal Bank.
National Merit Scholarship Semi-Finalist.

ACTIVITIES
Hobbies: Swimming, tennis, guitar.
Languages: Good command of French. Read Spanish.

REFERENCES
Available on request.

LOUISE CHAMBERS
ROUTE 9
BRENTWOOD, TENNESSEE   37027
(615) 371-6533

EDUCATION:

David Lipscomb College   Nashville, Tennessee
B.S. Art 1984   Minor: Literature

WORK HISTORY:

1981-Present   Freelance Illustrator
                    Brentwood Reporter and Star
                    Brentwood, Tennessee
                    Assisted in illustrating news stories, fashion
                    articles, human interest columns. Supplied
                    all the artwork for special edition of Sunday
                    magazine.

Summers 1980,   Office Assistant
  1981   Huntington Advertising Agency
                    Nashville, Tennessee
                    Receptionist, with some typing, filing, light
                    bookkeeping. Paste-ups/mechanicals when
                    needed.

References: On request

Charlotte Hopkins

Present Address:
28 Capen Street
Medford, MA 02155
617-395-0311

Permanent Address:
34 South Crescent
Maplewood, NJ 07040
201-761-1947

EDUCATION

1983 - present	TUFTS UNIVERSITY MEDFORD, MASSACHUSETTS A.B. in biology expected in 1984.
1980 - 1982	BOSTON UNIVERSITY BOSTON, MASSACHUSETTS Dean's List.
1977 - 1980	ACALANES HIGH SCHOOL LAFAYETTE, CALIFORNIA Symphonic Band Manager, Music Council Treasurer, District Honor Band, Student Board, California Scholarship Federation Life Member, California Girls' State Representative, Elks Club Most Valuable Student Scholarship - First Place Winner.

WORK EXPERIENCE

3/82 - present	WORD PROCESSOR OPERATOR The Electric Steno Input and output printing on Wang word processor.
9/81 - 12/81	WAITRESS/CASHIER Swenson's Restaurant
6/80 - 9/81	SECRETARY Estate in Probate of K.E. Ender, M.D. Bookkeeping, filing, letter writing.
9/79 - 12/79	GYMNASTICS COACH Lafayette Recreation Dept. Supervised junior high school teams, judged Interschool meets.
9/78 - 1/79	SECRETARY Doctors Medical Building Typing, filing, billing.
9/76 - 6/78	GYMNASTICS INSTRUCTOR Lafayette Gymnastics Taught 3 weekly classes of children grades K-6.

SKILLS

Typing - 60 WPM, Wang Word Processing, BASIC
and PL/C Computer Languages, Speak Spanish.

PERSONAL DATA

MAJOR INTEREST: Music, Gymnastics, Dance,
Drama.

TRAVEL

American Institute Choral Concert Tour of
Europe, 1976.

References Available on Request

Alice Marka
265 Main Street
Millburn, New Jersey 07641
(201) 691-1424

Education
1984   B.S. Biology
                            Williams College, Williamstown, Mass.

Employment
History:
1982-84   COMPUTER ANALYST
                            Data Systems, Inc.
                            Teaneck, NJ

                            Designed systems used in calculation media
                            for national elections. Assembled listings
                            for metal lengths, enforced number of feed-
                            throughs.

1981-1982   COMPUTER ANALYST
                            Compugraphics, Inc.
                            Newark, NJ

                            Job duties were similar to those in computer
                            analyst position—designed systems used in
                            media for national elections. Assembled
                            listings for metal lengths, capacities,
                            number of feedthroughs.

1980-1981   DESIGN AUTOMATION SPECIALIST
                            Educational Systems Co.
                            New York, NY

                            Debugged library and reading rooms. Wrote
                            functional and design specifications for
                            graphic layout editor/production manager.
                            Redesigned and provided support for data
                            base maintenance programs.

Availability: Free to travel and relocate
References: On request

RESUME

Robert Simpson   46 Claremont Street   Pittsburgh, Pa. 15219
(412) 362-1846

Education

1980-1984   B.S. Major: Biology   Minor: Chemistry
                       University of Miami, Miami, Fla.
                       3.4/4.0

Work History

Summer   SECRETARY/PARALEGAL
1982, 1983   Leeds, Smith, March, Pittsburgh, Pa.
                       Secretary to 2 estate attorneys: typing, steno,
                       general office, drafted wills, legal documents;
                       also research and proofreading.

Summer   GUY FRIDAY
1981   Career Blazers Employment Agency, New York, N.Y.
                       Generally assisted 2 placement managers: filed,
                       set up appointments, administered typing tests.

References: On request

Donald McOwen
846 Wendover Road
Danbury, Connecticut 06810
203-742-6879

Education:

1980-1984
Northwestern University, Chicago, Illinois
B.S. Chemistry / Math
Overall G.P.A. 3.6
Dean's List

Representative Course Work:
Chemistry, Analytical Chemistry, Organic Chemistry, Physical Chemistry, Thermodynamics, Algebra, Calculus, Differential Equations, Statistics, various courses in Russian, English, Philosophy and Psychology.

Work Experience:

Summer of 1982 & 1983
Trudy, Brown & Sons Insurance, Chicago, Ill.
Functioned as a secretary to three adjustors in bodily injury division: correspondence, sent out forms, ordered supplies, police reports, motor vehicle reports, set up physical exams, typed from dictaphone.

Summer of 1980
Chestnut Hill Country Club, Chicago, Illinois
Waiter

Honors/ Achievements:
Presidential Scholarship, Regents Scholarship Recipient Phi Beta Kappa.

Extracurricular Activities:
President of Debating Society, Member of Swimming Team.

Miscellaneous:
Willing to relocate and/or travel.

References:
Available on request.

Emory Bravian
315 Hudson Street
Scranton, Pennsylvania 06125
(717) 761-9283

Education:	
1979-1984	PhD., Chemistry
	Columbia College, New York City
1975-1979	B.A. Chemistry Major; Biology Minor
	New York University, New York City
Honors	Cumulative G.P.A. 3.61 (Index 4.0) Magna Cum Laude
	Phi Beta Kappa
Experience:	(While financing degree)
1979-1984	Driver/Attendant
	Acme Ambulance Service, Yonkers, New York
	Coordinated daily schedules, dispatched vehicles,
	attended patients.
1975-1984	Accounts Payable Clerk
	I.B.M., Yonkers, New York
	Diversified office duties in accounts payable
	department. Review bills and record all payments.
	Process sales invoices for billing.
	Research special assignments for treasurer and
	office manager.
Mobility:	Willing to relocate
References:	Furnished on request

Adrienne Koltman
2004 Kroley Street
Skokie, Illinois 60031
(312) 949-1649
XXXXXXX

Education:
1980-1984

B.A. Communications
State College of Illinois, Skokie, Ill.
G.P.A. 3.0

Work Experience:
1982-1984

Senior File Clerk
Hartford Insurance, Skokie, Ill.
Preparation of master file, responsible for
maintaining a file of 6,000 names, supervised
staff of 8 clerks. Trained new personnel.

1981-1982

Waiter
Jan's Coffee Shop & Diner, Skokie, Ill.
Waited on 60 tables lunch, dinner and supper,
functioned as bartender.

1980-1981

Dishwasher
Jan's Coffee Shop & Diner, Skokie, Ill.

References:

On request
XXXXXXX

MARSHA GLICK
14 Livingston Avenue
Yonkers, New York 10705
(914) 965-2825

EDUCATION:	Skidmore College, Saratoga Springs, New York (September 1979-May 1983) B.A. degree in Communications. Graduated with GPA of 3.51.
WRITING:	Co-authored A World Apart, Halcyon Press, Skidmore College.
	Wrote news and feature stories for the Skidmore College Journal.
	Published feature articles in Penguin magazine.
EDITING:	Served as Editor-in-Chief of 1982 Skidmore College yearbook. Planned organization and design of the book. Coordinated work of five editors, approved and edited all pictures and copy, worked with staff at all stages of production.
	Served as Editor-in-Chief of Yonkers High School Broadcaster.
LAYOUT/DESIGN:	Planned design scheme for 1982 college yearbook. Worked with layout editor on production of all layouts.
	Designed brochures for church youth conference.
	Earned 15 college credit hours in art.
PHOTOGRAPHY:	Shot, developed and printed pictures for college yearbook.
	Published pictures in Skidmore College Journal.
	Studied photography in college courses.
EMPLOYMENT:	Wrote news releases and did paste-up of brochures and pamphlets as assistant for Information Services, Skidmore College. (June-August 1982)
	Gathered class materials, and administered and graded tests as assistant to professor of philosophy, Skidmore College. (September-June 1981-82)
	Operated cash register as clerk for Skidmore College bookstore. (1979-82)
REFERENCES:	Furnished on request.

KATHRYN ALLAN

100 Stonehaven Drive
Boston, Massachusetts 02105
(617) 271-8432

CAREER
OBJECTIVE:
To secure an entry level position in the field of television production that will allow me to utilize my broadcasting and journalism skills.

EDUCATION:
Boston University College of Liberal Arts and Sciences
Boston, Massachusetts, 1983
B.A. Major: Communication Arts
Minor: English

BROADCASTING
EXPERIENCE:
BTV, Boston University Television, Boston, Massachusetts.
Summers 1982, 1981

Traffic and Continuity Manager: Responsible for every facet of traffic and continuity at BTV. Duties included the logging of commercials in individual productions and weekly programming tapes, overseeing the production of all commercials and PSAs, and reviewing all advertising copy.
Sales Representative: For BTV, selling air time to local businesses using rate card and contracts.
Producer: UP BEAT, weekly musical series for BTV.
Associate Director: WHO ME?, dramatic special for BTV.
Associate Director: PONDER THIS, information series for BTV.

Director, Associate Director, Technical Director, Audio Engineer, Electron Graphics, Stage Manager, ENG Equipment Operator, and Video Tape Editor--Various productions, September 1980-Present.

EMPLOYMENT:
May-September 1978, 1979
Marblehead Yacht Club, Marblehead, Massachusetts.
Head Life Guard, Swim Team Coach, and Swimming Instructor.
Responsible for life guard staff, scheduling, payroll, and purchasing pool supplies.

November 1979-May 1980
Filene's, Boston, Massachusetts
Retail Sales, Fine Jewelry Department

HONORS AND
MEMBERSHIPS:
Dean's List Boston University
Outstanding Senior Award 1983, BTV
Outstanding Entertainment Show 1982-UP BEAT
Outstanding Producer 1982-UP BEAT
Women in Communications, Boston University

REFERENCES:
Available on request.

Jonathan Mitchell
2 Parkchester Road
Wayland, Mass. 08426
(617) 358-1642

Education:
1984   University of Colorado, Boulder, Colo.
                    M.S. Computer Science, 1984

1983   Emerson College, Boston, Mass.
                    B.S. Computer Science

Honors:
1983   Magna Cum Laude, Phi Beta Kappa

Work History:
1982-1983   Computer Operator
                    Makin Systems, Wayland, Mass.
                    Developed software package for PDP for management
                    and analysis of database.
                    Developed query languages to select records for
                    Barlean System.

1981-1982   Systems Programmer
                    Made various efficiency improvements in the
                    National Election Program. Designed performance
                    improvements.

References: On request

RÉSUMÉ OF LAURIE ADAMS

ADDRESS
24 Oak Park Road
Peekskill, New York 11304
(914) 341-4416

EDUCATION
1981
to
Present
MEREDITH COLLEGE, Yorktown Heights, New York
Candidate for a Bachelor of Science degree in
Computer Information Systems.

1982
PRIME COMPUTER, INC., Framingham, Massachusetts
Attended Prime Customer Education session in Computer
Operations.

1981
DIGITAL EQUIPMENT CORPORATION, Bedford, Massachusetts
Attended Digital Customer Education session in Compu-
ter Operations.

HARDWARE/
SOFTWARE
DECsystem 1060   TOPS - 10
PRIME 850, 750   Primos/ Information
SYCOR 405

PROFESSIONAL
EXPERIENCE
1981
to
Present
BAINBRIDGE MANUFACTURING, Yorktown Heights, New York

Computer Operator
Duties include operation of DEC 1060 and PRIME 850
computer system; resolving computer control messages
when required; independently managing operator's
functions, such as loading tapes, cards, disk packs,
and paper; perform system backups and user retrievals;
monitor and control user job traffic.

1979
to
1981
SKLAR SYSTEMS, Peekskill, New York

Production Control Assistant
Responsible for manufacturing production control including material control, production scheduling, WIP
inventory records, planning, and expediting.

* Project Assistant on MRP Project: Implemented
and maintained MRP System, including Item
Master File, control data, and transaction data.

Purchasing/Production Control Secretary
Handled complete range of secretarial duties.

* Promoted to Production Control Assistant.

REFERENCES
Furnished upon request.

Theresa Vitulli
21 Brite Avenue
Scarsdale, New York 10583
(914) 555-7336

EDUCATION

1983
Katherine Gibbs School, New York.
ENTREE Program

1979-1983
Bachelor of Arts, Union College, Schenectady, New York.
Major in Drama. Minor in Psychology

1978-1979
Richmond College, London, England.
Audition Acceptance Program affiliated with The Royal Academy of Dramatic
Arts

ABILITIES

typewriting---50 words a minute
shorthand--80 words a minute; knowledge of bookkeeping, filing;
training in business writing, telephone techniques, and operation
of IBM computer and Xerox machines.

EXPERIENCE

1983   Kaplan-Sandercock, Inc., New York
  Position: Interior Design Assistant. Part-time employment.

1983   Union College: Improvisation
  Position: Teaching Assistant

1982   Krebs, Stengel & Co., Inc., New York
  Position: Showroom salesperson; General office work.   Summer
  employment and part-time employment

1980-81   Cooperative Dance Association of Westchester
  Position: Assistant Dance Teacher to Ms Rita Chazen.
  Part-time employment

1979   Alvin Ailey Dance Company. Scholarship Candidate

PERSONAL

Appeared in or directed 5 major productions at Union College. Widely
travelled in Europe. Photographer.

REFERENCES

Available on request.

David Iramen
39 Stanford Avenue
Milford, Ohio   45208
(513) 862-4759

Education: 1981-1983	Northwestern University, Chicago, Illinois M.A. Theatre Major; Music Minor Overall GPA 3.6 Dean's List
1979-1981	University of Chicago, Chicago, Illinois B.A. Theatre Major; Music Minor
Work Experience: 1981-1983	Publicity Assistant American Diabetes Assoc. Responsible for gathering information to establish chapters. Duties included general secretarial and clerical duties, handling of news releases and contact with chapter members.
1980-1981	Receptionist Warwick & Legler Greeted visitors; handled switchboard
Northwestern Achievements:	National Presidential Scholarship Recipient; Alpha Sigma Phi; National Debating Society Sigma Delta Sigma; National Theatre Society, Alpha Beta Nu.
References:	Available on request

Julia Harrison
18 Hamilton Avenue
Lawrence, New York 11559
(516) 886-9071

Education

Lehman College, City University of N.Y.
B.A. Cum Laude   June, 1983
Major: Economics
Minor: English

Honors: Omicron Delta Epsilon - National Economics
          Honor Society
          Intramural Tennis Champion

Employment

Hamilton Peabody and Company   New York, New York
Intern 9/82 - 6/83
Participated in standard accounting, budgeting
process, variance analysis, credit approval,
management of bank balances and short-term money
management.

Eastern Savings Bank   Bronx, New York
Administrative Assistant 6/82 - 9/82
Provided financial data to commercial account officers.

Skills

Type 55 WPM

References

Provided upon request

Marjorie Glenn
6 North St.
Byron, Pa. 16917
(814) 362-0963

Education
1984   A.A. in English
                        Swiftwater College, Easton, Pa.

Employment History
1982-1984   SALES CLERK
                        Parker Auto Parts, Easton, Pa.
                        Responsible for all sales in auto parts.
                        Trained sales staff, checked inventory,
                        ordered stock, designed showroom.

1981-1984   INTERVIEWER
                        The Pulse, New York City
                        Interviewed families re new products; trained
                        and supervised new staff members.

Hobbies   Swimming, archery, skiing

References   On request

JAMES L. ROTH

_____
_____

PRESENT ADDRESS
493 Fairfield Beach Road
Fairfield, Connecticut 06430
(203) 665-2154

HOME ADDRESS
Sunset Beach Road
Sag Harbor, New York 11936
(516) 973-5454

PERSONAL SUMMARY   Presently a senior English major at Fairfield University and expect to graduate in May 1983. Through full and part-time employment, as noted below, have been able to pay for 40% of my college expenses. My personal qualities include leadership skills, initiative, reliability, and a determined and optimistic outlook on life. I am well traveled and experienced at working with people in a variety of different social as well as professional levels.

EDUCATION
. B.A. Fairfield University, May 1983
. Major - English
. Arranged curriculum to include 9 credits in marketing and 12 credits in communications.

EMPLOYMENT
HISTORY

The American Hotel, Sag Harbor, New York. (1982)
Responsibilities included general service and coordination activities.

Seaview Auto Parts Corp., Bridgeport, Connecticut.
(1981-82)
Responsible for inventory control, shipping and receiving, and tax computations.

Exxon Service Station, Fairfield, Connecticut. (1981)
Service attendant-responsible for second shift operation in manager's absence.

The Long Wharf Restaurant, Sag Harbor, New York. (1979-81)
Accountable for a variety of operational functions; progressed into a supervisory position responsible for several employees and the management of large sums of money.

Campus Food Service (Mackie), Fairfield University. (1980)
Service Operator.

ACTIVITIES
Manager - Fairfield University Mens' Glee Club
Registration Committee Member - Chairman, 1983
Orientation Committee Member
Fairfield University Students' Association Member
Commencement Committee Member

REFERENCES   Furnished upon request.

Ronald Towe
1265 Lakeview Rd.
New Philadelphia, Ohio 44663
(216) 555-6784

EDUCATION:

1983 B.A. English/University of Notre Dame/GPA 3.4

JOB TARGET:

Editor's Assistant

SCHOOL ACTIVITIES:

. Published short fiction in school magazines and literary reviews

. Edited copy for Scholastic magazine

. Interviewed Independent President Candidate Harold Stassen for Scholastic magazine

. Reviewed films for school newspapers

. Arranged Independent Study for novel writing

. Organized workshops for authors at Sophomore Literary Festival

. Tutored juvenile delinquents at South Bend Correctional Home for Boys

. Instructed retarded youths at Logan Center

. Played interhall tennis

. Ran interhall track

SUMMER WORK EXPERIENCE:

. Title researcher for attorneys Fitzpatrick and Zimmerman

. Reclamation laborer at Mudsock Mines

. Plant laborer at PepsiCo. Bottling Company

. Roller-guard at United Skates of America

REFERENCES:

. Available upon Request

Susan Stacks
39 Shadow Drive
Cherry Hill, N.J.
(609) 682-9403

EDUCATION

Montclair State College,
Upper Montclair, New Jersey
B.A., English - May 1983
GPA 4.0

HONORS

Dean's List 1979-1983
General Excellence Award 1979-1983
Elected to Who's Who Among American
College and University Students

WORK EXPERIENCE

May to September 1979-1983
Neighbor News, Cherry Hill, New Jersey
Reporter, News/Editorial Department
(internship)

January to May 1981
Montclair State College, Public
Relations Department.
Copywriter, General Assistant
(internship)

STUDENT ACTIVITIES

Literary Editor, The Unicorn, college
yearbook, 1982-1983
Class Senator 1981-1982
Tutor, Writing Center 1980-1982

SPECIAL SKILLS

Type 50 WPM
Operate Video Display Terminal

Nancy Oakes
45 Center Street
Rockville Center, N.Y. 11575
(516) 764-2413

CAREER GOALS   Editorial or Production Assistant

EDUCATION   Adelphi University, Garden City, New York
                      B.A. 1984
                      Major: English   Minor: Films
                      3.4 out of 4.0

WORK EXPERIENCE
Summer 1983   Gal Friday
                      Miller Advertising Agency, Garden City, N.Y.
                      Responsible for editing and proofreading
                      catalogues and flyers. Some receptionist
                      duties, heavy phones; typing, fast longhand.

Summer 1982   Accounts Receivable Clerk
                      Garden City Golf & Country Club, Garden City, N.Y.
                      Responsibilities included heavy computer work on
                      a Basic Four System. Daily processing of charges
                      to members' accounts, light bookkeeping, bank
                      reconciliation and some accounts payable.

Summer 1981   CRT Operator
                      Long Island Collections Agency, Garden City, N.Y.
                      Processed form letters into a CRT system to be
                      mailed to delinquent accounts.

LANGUAGES   Fluent French; knowledge of Spanish.

PERSONAL INTERESTS   Films, sculpturing, travel, gourmet cooking.

REFERENCES   Available on request.

Edith Paulette
562 Ridge Lane
Danbury, Connecticut 06810
(203) 742-1605

Education:

M.A. 1984
Major English Literature, Minor French
New York University, New York City

B.A. 1982
Major English, Minor Psychology
Barnard College, New York City

Work History:
Summer, 1984

Capitol Records, Inc., New York City
Computer Operative
Position included processing of daily production jobs
such as inventory reports, general ledger, accounts
receivable, accounts payable. Complete training on an
IBM 370-135, D.O.S. System.

Summer, 1983

Secretary
Doubleday, New York City
Secretary to senior editor, took dictation, bonded
own correspondence, typed manuscripts, contact with
authors, set up meetings.

Summer, 1982

Cashier/Sales
Maximes Department Stores, Albany, New York
Processed all cash purchases. Became familiar with
stock for all departments to assist customers in
shopping. Supervised trainees. Assisted manager with
sales promotions.

Skills:

Typing 65 wpm
Fluency in French, reading knowledge of Italian

References:

Available upon request

Linda Schneider
9 Gedney Terrace
White Plains, New York 10708
(914) 772-1134

EDUCATION:

Sept. 1979 - May 1983

State University of New York
College at Purchase

Bachelor of Arts
Literature

WORK HISTORY:

Feb. 1980 - Present

Reference Clerk (part-time)

Yonkers Public Library
1500 Central Park Ave., Yonkers, N.Y.

Assisting patrons with research,
answering phones, light typing,
clerical duties.

Summers

Arts and Crafts Counselor

1981   Summer Pines Day Camp New Rochelle, N.Y.
1980   Mosholu Day Camp Spring Valley, N.Y.
1979   Arrowhead Day Camp Scarsdale, N.Y.
1978   Arrowhead Day Camp Scarsdale, N.Y.

Plan crafts program for campers, order
supplies, instruct campers

PERSONAL DATA:

Enjoy writing, working with people, have
submitted two children's books for
possible publication

Portfolio and References available upon request.

SUSAN JONES
77 E. 92nd Street Apt. 2
New York, New York 10027
(212) 368-3633

EDUCATION

Pratt/Phoenix School of Design, New York, New York
Program in graphic design, 1982-1983

Amherst College, Amherst, Massachusetts
B.A., English and Art History, 1981

Harvard University, Cambridge, Massachusetts
Junior Year 1979-1980

WORK EXPERIENCE

Associate Editor. Matthew Bender & Co., New York, New York,
legal book publishers. Coordinated production of U.S. Tax
Week, a weekly tax magazine, as well as edited, proofread,
and laid out the publication. 10/81 - 7/82

Arts Intern. Boston Phoenix, Boston, Massachusetts. Edited
and proofread copy for the Arts section of this weekly newspaper (circulation 75,000). Compiled calendar of fine arts,
music, and theatre events. 6/80 - 8/80

Research Assistant. Boston Museum of Fine Arts, Boston, Massachusetts.
Researched information for the museum's slide collection and
publications. 1/80 - 5/80; 6/78 - 8/78

Advertising Assistant. WBOS Radio Station, Boston, Massachusetts.
Edited advertising copy for commercial broadcast. 6/78 - 8/78

EXTRACURRICULAR

Layout Staff. Olio, Amherst College. Assisted in layout and production of college yearbook. 1/79 - 5/79, 1/81 - 5/81

Production Staff. Seventh Sister, Harvard University. Edited and
proofread copy as well as worked on layout design for monthly
magazine published by Harvard/Radcliffe women. Magazine includes
news, feature articles, and art. 9/79 - 5/80

Tutor. Cambridge School Volunteers' Project, Cambridge, Massachusetts.
Tutored high school children on a one-to-one basis in math and
English. 12/79 - 5/80

PERSONAL

Enjoy drawing, painting, and writing fiction and poetry.
Have travelled through Europe and Asia.
Played varsity tennis and squash at Amherst College.
Have reading and speaking knowledge of French.

References on Request

George De Palma
66 Midchester Avenue
White Plains, New York 10606
Telephone: (914) 946-1925

OBJECTIVE

To obtain full-time employment with a progressive company utilizing my unique educational background and work experiences where responsibility may lead to top management level.

EDUCATION

University of Dayton School of Law 1982-1983
Dayton, Ohio 45469
Completed Courses In: Contracts, Civil Procedure, Criminal Law, Legal Research and Writing, Property, Constitutional Law, Torts and Moot Court.

Villanova University
Villanova, Pa. 19085
B.A. English 1982; Dean's List, 3.47 in Major
Tony Lema Golf Scholarship

EMPLOYMENT

1981-82	Resident Assistant, Villanova, Pa. 19085 Responsible for 300 residents in a dorm.
1980-82	File Clerk for Patent Law Firm David Hoxie Faithfull & Hapgood General filing duties.
1980	Security Guard, Gleason Security A. T. & T. Plant, Hartsdale, N.Y. Nighttime shift.
1979	Stock Clerk, Callan Furniture, Inc., White Plains, N.Y. Inventory, stock and maintenance.
1977-78	Sportswriter, Westchester Rockland Newspapers, Harrison, N.Y. Covered high school basketball and football games; some proofreading and re-write.
1978	Sportswriter, Suburban Street News, White Plains, N.Y. Covered local sports news, interviewed athletes; some proofreading.

INTERESTS:

Writing, Sports, Numismatics, People

Willing to relocate.

References will be furnished upon request.

JOANNE CANADRY   5918 Sunny Drive
                                        Las Vegas, Nevada 89120
                                        (702) 451-2839

EDUCATION
    University of Nevada, Las Vegas, Nevada, 1979-1983
    B.A. - Geography, Minor - Geology
    Magna Cum Laude

PROJECTS AND INTERNSHIPS (1980 - 1983)

    . Land Use Survey via aerial photo interpretation; Ground
      truth checking. District Regional Planning Commission,
      Las Vegas.

    . Satellite image and air photo interpretation. Cartographic
      products via computer, photo/mechanical and manual tech-
      niques; University of Nevada.

    . Compiled, designed and produced a map of Nevada Mineral
      Occurrences, Las Vegas, Nevada.

    . Identified and organized mineral specimens, Las Vegas
      Cultural Center, Las Vegas, Nevada.

    . Volunteer - Nevada Geological Observatory - organized map
      data.

SPECIAL SKILLS

    Cartography: graphic design, computer mapping, drafting,
    dark room techniques, color separation and printing,
    shooting and developing film.

    Remote Sensing: digital image processing, statistical
    data analysis, manual interpretation of satellite imagery.

    Geology: Knowledge of landforms, rocks and minerals.

    Clerical: typing, billing, ordering, phones.

EMPLOYMENT

Present   General Office Duties, I.P.O. Assoc.,
(Part-Time)   Las Vegas

              Medical Assistant/Receptionist,
              Dr. George Thompson, Las Vegas

1978-1982   Office Receptionist, Library Communication System -
              University Library, Las Vegas

1977-1978   Ordering/Shipping, Hunter Publishing Co., Las Vegas

References upon request

SUSAN McDERMOTT

211 E. 38th Street   Coleman Street
New York, New York 10016   Woodridge, New York 12789
Tel: (212) 725-1245   Tel: (914) 434-7235

EDUCATION

Bachelor of Arts, History Education (1983)
S.U.N.Y. at Cortland, Cortland, New York

EXPERIENCE

May 1983-
Present   Assistant Buyer for Domestics, Sullivan's Department Stores.
                 Assisting in the purchasing of domestics, responsible for
                 the merchandising of products, taking of inventories,
                 setting up work schedules, and other daily responsibilities.

1979-1982
University   Librarian Assistant and Supervisor, Cortland Memorial
Semesters   Library, responsible for training and supervising students,
                 filing, typing, cataloging, and record keeping.

1982-
Summer   Waitress, Kaplan's Delicatessen, primary responsibility
                 training waitresses along with traditional waitress duties.

1979-1980
Summers   Waitress, Howard Johnson's Restaurant, training waitresses,
                 cashier, and regular duties.

ADDITIONAL INFORMATION

*Travelled to Ireland, Mexico, California, and West Coast of the United
States. These experiences have been beneficial in learning how to
communicate with people in different types of situations and environments.

REFERENCES FURNISHED UPON REQUEST

Naomi Martin
300 Allen Avenue
Pittsburgh, Pennsylvania
(412) 961-8376

Career Objective: Entry-level position as a paralegal with corporation or law firm.

Education: B.A., 1982 University of Chicago, Chicago, Ill.
Major: History   Minor: Spanish

Paralegal Certificate, Adelphi University
Garden City, New York, 1983

Employment:

Summer of '83   Legal Secretary, Deutch & Morgan, Pittsburgh, Pa.
Functioned as a legal secretary/assistant to a partner in antitrust and international corporate specialization, full secretarial responsibilities, some research, heavy client contact, thorough knowledge of legal document drafts, SEC filings and registration statements.

Summer of '82   Receptionist, Marshall & Mattel, Pittsburgh, Pa.
Greeted clients, answered call-director, responsible for overflow typing.

Summer of '81   Salesperson, Martha's Boutique, Milford, Pa.
Waited on customers, handled cash register, credit cards, in charge of inventory.

Languages: Fluency in Spanish, reading knowledge of French.

Interests: Swimming, Horseback riding, Tennis

References: On request.

Margaret Foster
210 Maple Street
Arlington, Va. 22205
(703) 874-1643

Education:
1979-1983   B.A. Journalism Major; Spanish Minor
                   George Washington University, Washington, D.C.

Honors:
1982-1983   Dean's List

Experience:
1982-1983   "Woman's Wear Weekly", Washington, D.C.
                   Research assistant to consumer reporter.
                   Filled in as a copy aide; assisted in pro-
                   duction of news and fashion show. 1982
                   Election Eve, worked at United Press Interna-
                   tional, reporting to stations with latest
                   returns on congressional and senatorial
                   elections.

1981 (summer)   "Show Magazine", Washington, D.C.
                   Worked as editorial assistant to executive
                   editor. Duties included coordination of or-
                   ganized system of manuscript flow between
                   editors and assisted in copyediting and proof-
                   reading copy. Assisted in rewriting news and
                   planning news stories and layouts.

1980 (summer)   "Main Street", Arlington, Va.
                   Assistant to fashion editor. Covered and re-
                   ported on fashion shows. Assisted in writing,
                   editing, reporting and layout for local daily
                   newspaper. Published original material.
                   Proofreading and editing copy. Liaison with
                   production department.

Skills: Fluent in Spanish
References: On request

Victoria Branderling
315 Federal Street
Glendale, New York 11385
(718) 619-9246

Education:
1984   A.A. in Landscape Engineering
                        Tifton College, Cleveland, Ohio

Employment
History:
1982-1983   Paralegal--Ace & Gottlieb, New York City
                        functioned as legal researcher estates division
                        major law firm-research, contracts, prepared cases
                        for before trial evaluation, court notes, dictation,
                        typing, coordinated daily schedule

1981-1982   Assist bookkeeper--A.C. Nelson, New York City
                        processed all orders for payments, in charge of
                        inventory, receipts, cash transactions, bookkeeping
                        through general ledger payments, taxes

1980-1981   Figure Clerk--Kenyon & Eckhardt, New York City
                        In charge checking all bills, receipts, deposits.
                        Processed sales invoices for billing, assisted
                        special assignments for controller, office manager

References: On request

Carol Richmond
23 James Street
Yonkers, N.Y. 10763
(914) 965-4416

EDUCATION

1984   B.A. Major in Spanish; Minor in Italian
                     Seton College, Yonkers, N.Y.

EMPLOYMENT HISTORY

Summer   Secretary
1983   State Farm Insurance, Yonkers, N.Y.
                     Assisted two adjusters; heavy phone contact, typing,
                     filing, dictaphone.

Summer   Receptionist
1982, 1981   Dr. Paul Smith, Yonkers, N.Y.
                     Greeted patients, responsible for billing,
                     wrote receipts.

EXTRACURRICULAR ACTIVITIES

1983   President, National Spanish Club

LANGUAGES   Fluent Spanish and Italian

SKILLS   Typing 65 wpm

REFERENCES   Available on request

Phyllis Dorfman
27 Triangle Street
Charlotte, S.C. 29565
(803) 661-6240

Career Objective:
   Position with Tartiene 500 Company as Translator & Management
   Trainee.

Education:

1982-1984	M.A. French Major, Spanish Minor University of Ohio, Cleveland, Ohio
1978-1982	B.A. French Major, Spanish Minor Russell Sage College, Troy, New York

Work History:

1982-1984	Nursing Assistant, Cleveland General Hospital, Cleveland, Ohio. Responsible for patient care in Intensive Care Unit.
Summer, 1981	Assistant Coordinator, First Aid Station, Cape Cod Inn, Cape Cod, Mass. Aided attending physician at summer resort. Managed inventory supply and assisted in routine medical procedure. Demonstrated first aid techniques to guests at the inn.
Summer, 1980	Administrative Assistant, Boston Hospital, Boston, Mass. Typing, telephone and information referrals. Handled heavy paper work and managed work flow between departments.

Skills: Typing
                 Dictaphone

References: Available on request

Maria T. Gonzales
560 Attala Drive
Bakersfield, California 93309

(805) 651-3987

Job Objective:	Programmer Trainee
Education	1984 B.S. degree from University of California
	Mathematics Major - Business studies and computer training
	Activities - Advertising Manager of campus newspaper
	Volunteer hospital work

Experience

1984-present   Atlas Electronics - Bakersfield, California
                    Computer Operator

                    Operates and monitors digital computer equipment
                    (370-155 and 360-65). Follows established programs
                    and new programs under development. Selects
                    appropriate processing devices (card, tape, disc)
                    and loads computer. Observes lights on console and
                    storage devices to report deviations from standards.

                    Maintains records of job performance; checks and
                    maintains controls on each job. Solves operational
                    problems and checks out new programs; assists in
                    making necessary corrections. Assists less ex-
                    perienced operators.

1980-1984   Bee Newspaper - Modesto, California
(part-time)   Bookkeeper/Clerk Typist

                    Typed invoices, posted and maintained records and
                    files; made and verified computations. Typed
                    classified ads and sent to composing department.

References   Provided on request.

Bob McGowen
261 Baker Street
Chicago, Illinois 60698
(312) 351-6671

Education:
1980-1984   Oberlin College, Oberlin, Ohio
                     B.A. Music: Music Therapy and Piano

Honors: G.P.A. 3.6
                     Magna Cum Laude
                     Phi Beta Kappa

Employment:
1982-1984   SALESMAN
                     Cloche's Piano Studio, Oberlin, Ohio
                     Demonstrated piano for customers

1980-1982   SELF-EMPLOYED PIANO TEACHER
                     Taught piano to individual students

Skills: In addition to piano, play harp, guitar, violin and
                     drums

References: Available on request

JANICE MORGAN
201 W. 81st Street, Apt. 5R
New York, New York 10024
(212) 724-9284

EDUCATION

Vassar College, Poughkeepsie, New York
B.A. in Philosophy, May 1983
Additional course work in History and English
Senior Essay: "Prostitution; A Study in Social Morality and the Law."

The Madeira School, Greenway, Virginia
Graduated May, 1979

WORK EXPERIENCE

The Washington Post Company: Clerk, Advertising Dept.
Summer, 1981
    Responsible for preparing advertisements to run daily.
    Worked with layout and paste-up crews. Clerical liaison
    between Advertising Sales and Production Staffs.

Merrill Photo Supply: Floor Clerk
Winter, 1978
    Sold, ordered and serviced cameras. Sales Assistant.

VOLUNTEER INTERNSHIPS

The Department of Human Resources.
1978-1979
    Worked with government social worker, assisted with court
    and case work for children placed in foster homes.

Congressional Intern: The Hon. John M. Slack (D. W.VA.)
Office Volunteer. 1977 - 1978
    Researched bills and constituent requests.

Childrens Hospital: (Washington D.C.) Operating Room
Clerical Assistant. 1976 - 1977
    Observed major surgery and recorded operating statistics.

ACTIVITIES

The Miscellany News: Weekly Student Newspaper.

Managing Editor: Recruited and maintained staff of writers,
artists and photographers. Edited and proofread copy.
Supervised layout and production of each issue. Editorial
writer. 1981 - 1982

Photography Editor: Responsible for developing, printing
and assigning photographs for each issue. Assisted with
production. Contributing writer 1979 - 1980

Vassarion: Student Yearbook. Contributing Photographer, 1983

Captain: Intramural Waterpolo team, 1983

INTERESTS

Creative writing, whitewater rafting and photography.
Traveled extensively in France during summers of 1976, 1977
and 1978.

REFERENCES

Available on request.

James Evans

62 Summers Road
Fairfield, CT 06430
(203) 374-4156

EDUCATION:
1984   B.S. in Physics
                        Connecticut College, New London, CT.

WORK EXPERIENCE:
Summer   Laboratory Technician
1983   U.S. Coast Guard, Fairfield, CT.
                        Participated in joint project with Coast Guard and
                        Connecticut College Physics Advisory Board in an
                        experiment using a nuclear particle accelerator.
                        Responsible for all Geiger counter measurements.

Summer   Guy Friday
1982   Smith & Leeds Real Estate, Ft. Lauderdale, FL.
                        General office work: set up appointments, interviewed
                        potential buyers and sellers. Studied toward and
                        received a Florida Real Estate License.

Summer   Sales Clerk
1981   Motor Clinic, Avon, CT.
                        Reorganized and consolidated auto parts operation,
                        inventory control.

REFERENCES: On request.

Helen Hanerford
29 Rockland Ave.
Hartford, Conn. 06131
(203) 362-1415

Education:
1980-1984   B.A. Political Science
                       Yale, New Haven, Conn.
Honors: G.P.A. 3.5
                       Dean's List
Activities:
1982-1984   Yale University Black Student Service Center.
                       Coordinated Social Affairs, Public Relations, and
                       Educational and Technical Services.
Experience:
1983-1984   TELLER
                       National Bank of Conn., New Haven, Conn.
                       Trained and evaluated teller trainees. Performed
                       all commercial bank teller functions. Prepared
                       branch currency reports on a daily basis. Acted
                       as service specialist for City, State and Federal
                       Government employees to expedite check cashing.
                       Light typing to assist clearance teller.
1981-1983   CASHIER SALES
                       Bullock's Department Store, New Haven, Conn.
                       Processed all cash purchases. Responsible for pre-
                       paration of weekly sales, mark all merchandise, prepare
                       list of sales items, work with ad agency on appropriate
                       ads, wait on customers, assist in customer relations,
                       preparation for new charge accounts.
Summer, 1981   CLERK
                       Haskins & Rick, New Haven, Conn.
                       General secretarial duties including preparation of
                       cases for trial, drafting of legal documents, legal
                       research.
Interests: Theatre, reading, chess
References: On request

<u>MICHAEL TOWNER</u>

125 Lyndon Way, Newark, N.J. 07814   (201) 994-6295

<u>Education:</u>

    B.A., George Washington University, Washington, D.C. June, '84.
          Major: Political Science   Minor: French

<u>Experience:</u>

    (Part-time while in school, full-time during summer)

Oct. '80 - present   ASSISTANT TO PUBLIC RELATIONS DIRECTOR,
                        Planned Parenthood, Washington, D.C.
                        Responsibility for planning, researching
                        and typing news releases, set up press,
                        radio and TV interviews for staff;
                        function as editorial, production
                        assistant on newsletter. Prepare
                        material to reach various international
                        chapters; make travel arrangements and
                        assist in setting up conferences; co-
                        ordinate special events; secretarial
                        duties.

<u>Skills:</u>

                        Thorough knowledge of office procedure,
                        dictaphone, IBM electronic typewriter
                        (75 wpm), word processing, filing, call
                        director, switchboard, etc.

<u>Languages:</u>

                        Fluency in French, reading knowledge of Spanish

<u>References:</u>

                        Available on request.

MICHAEL KLEIN
41 Del Rey Drive
Mt. Vernon, N.Y. 10552
(914-667-4598)

Education: Moravian College, Bethlehem, Pa., Graduated May, 1983
                  B.A. Political Science and B.A. Journalism

Employment: June - December 1983 Employed full time with American
                  Investors Group, Houston, as Marketing Representative
                  working with a supporting staff of six. Knowledge of
                  financial annuity planning.

Summer   1982 Aarco Refrigeration Company. In charge of entire
Employment: Hershey ice cream account. Responsibilities included
                  employing and controlling drivers for delivery trucks.

                  1981 Exxon Station in Pennsylvania. Employed as gas
                  attendant/mechanic.

                  1980 - 1981 U.S. Army Reserve. Served as a Second
                  Lieutenant in charge of over forty soldiers. Received
                  honorable discharge in June of 1980.

                  1979 - 1980 Barclay's Bank of New York. Teller in
                  foreign exchange transactions and travellers checks.

                  1978 Windels, Marx, Davies & Ives, law firm.
                  Clerk/Messenger for firm. Duties included travelling the
                  East Coast serving legal papers and handling large amounts
                  of cash.

                  1977 Camp Fordham, N.Y. Held dual position of lifeguard
                  and counselor. In charge of over 20 teenagers.

Activities   College: Executive director, Student Society for
and   International Relations; President, Students for Political
Interests: and Economic Consciousness; Pledgemaster Recording
                  Secretary, and Elections Officer, Beta Lambda Chi;
                  Advertising Editor and Reporter, the Comenian;
                  Editor-in-Chief, The Underground Press. Worked actively
                  with local printer, reproduction; and sold space to finance
                  paper.

                  High School: New York Military Academy. Bronze and Gold
                  Superintendent's medal, Gold Medal in European History and
                  Economics, Directors Cup, Steeplechase trophy, Executive
                  Lieutenant, Varsity Swim Team, and Varsity Riding Squad.

ALICE EDWARDS   740 East Gun Hill Road   Bronx, NY   10467   (212) 555-9084

OBJECTIVE: Management training position leading ultimately to
                upper-level management

EDUCATION: Tufts University, Medford, MA
                1983-BS, Psychology-Mental Health

                Dean's List
                Federal Mental Health Grant Recipient
                Mary Bethune Social Science Award Nominee

                Served as receptionist in Department of Admissions,
                Sophomore year
                Career Guidance and Placement Center, Junior year
                Dormitory Representative
                Member of Psychology Society
                Member of Afro-American Society

EXPERIENCE:

                HEALTH INSURANCE PLAN, New York, NY

5/82-9/82   Administrative assistant
                • Maintained enrollment reports; updated admissions
                  records for Department of Mental Health

                • Did statistical analysis for Directors' quarterly
                  reports; performed secretarial functions

5/81-9/81   Census Taker
                • Collected data from 60 doctors; performed statistical
                  analysis for HEW-sponsored Medicare time study

                • Conducted survey in HIP medical centers in Brooklyn,
                  Queens and Bronx

5/80-9/80   Medical Assistant
                • Organized record room for greater efficiency;
                  corrected all misfiling

                • Made appointments; maintained patient files;
                  completed non-medical inf)rmation on Med 10's; called
                  patients for follow-up

VOLUNTEER EXPERIENCE:

9/82-5/83   Mental Health Counselor - BAYCOVE CHILDREN'S CENTER,
                Boston, MA
                • Managed day treatment center for emotionally
                  disturbed children; planned special-oriented
                  activities, developed curriculum and taught children
                  - degree credit

SKILLS: Excellent organizer; relate well at all levels; type
                50 WPM

REFERENCES ON REQUEST

BERNARD HUGHES
18 Fenimore Road
Scarsdale, New York 10583
(914) 723-9540

EDUCATION   Union College   Schenectady, New York
                 Bachelor of Arts
                 Major: Psychology

EXPERIENCE   Shamrock and Cook, Inc.
                 Interior Design Assistant

                 Blue Monday, Inc.
                 Salesperson

SKILLS   Typing--50 WPM; shorthand--80 WPM.
                 Knowledge of bookkeeping, filing.
                 Trained in business writing, telephone
                 techniques, and operation of IBM computer
                 and Xerox machines.

REFERENCES   Provided on request.

Beverly Sanders
40 St. Clare's St.
Tucson, Arizona 85721
(602) 814-9002

<u>Education</u>:

1980-1984   B.A. Psychology
Arizona State University, Tempe, Arizona

<u>Work History</u>:   <u>Chanticler Advertising, Inc</u>.

1982-1984   Tempe, Arizona
As secretary to account executive took dictation,
set up meetings, checked copy, proofread advertising
promotions

1980-1982   <u>Career Blazers Temporary Personnel, Inc</u>.
As temporary gal Friday, assignments included A.B.C.,
London Records, Lark Foundations, Carnegie Endowment
for Peace.

<u>Skills</u>:   Typing 75 wpm, steno
Knowledge of French

<u>Mobility</u>:   Willing to travel or relocate

<u>References</u>:   On request

Business

JESSICA DORMAN
28 Rose Avenue
Kirkwood, Missouri 63122
(314) 653-9271

EDUCATION

Community College   St. Louis, Missouri
B.S., Accounting 1983
GPA 3.75

EMPLOYMENT
1980 to
present

(while financing degree)
Koehler Manufacturing Company St. Louis,
Missouri
Accounting Clerk
Handle basic accounting transactions, code
invoices for proper distribution, classify
transactions and process warehouse invoices

1978 to
1980

Brook and Howe, St. Louis, Missouri
Accounting Clerk
Assisted in general accounting procedures
Analyzed and interpreted statements and
reports

MOBILITY

Willing to relocate

REFERENCES

Forwarded upon request

June Anderson
65 Vermont Avenue
Augusta, Maine 04330
(207) 682-5967

Education:
1980 - 1984   University of Minnesota
                              St. Paul, Minnesota
                              Major: Business   Minor: Accounting

Experience:
5/83 - 8/83   Accounting Clerk
                              Hartford Insurance Co.
                              Augusta, Maine

Responsible for accounts payable, accounts receivable, daily bank deposits;
handled credit collection correspondence, collection calls, relieved receptionist, general office duties.

5/82 - 8/82   Proofreader
                              Johnson Advertising Agency
                              Augusta, Maine

All around Gal-Friday in creative department, major responsibilities
included proofreading, editing, typing copy for print, radio, TV media;
light bookkeeping duties.

5/81 - 8/81   Clerk Typist
                              Kenmore Printing Inc.
                              Augusta, Maine

Diversified office duties in accounts payable department: processed sales
invoices, typed bills.

Reference: Available from Placement Office
                              University of Minnesota
                              St. Paul, Minnesota 55149
                              (612) 654-1367

Daniel Michaels
410 Rugby Rd.
Scarsdale, NY 10410
(914) SC 5-3214

PROFESSIONAL OBJECTIVE:	To obtain an entry-level position in the financial or accounting corporate sector, with growth opportunity for advancement to management.
EDUCATION:	**MERCY COLLEGE** Bachelor of Science in Business Administration, with a specialization in Finance. May, 1985 Cum 3.109
WORK EXPERIENCE: 3/82 - Present	**PRIVATE ELECTRICIAN'S ASSISTANT** John Tracey, Scarsdale, N.Y. Responsible for proper assistance in wiring and pipework; installation of ceiling fans and air-conditioning.
SUMMER 1981	**TRUCK DRIVER** Mutual Biscuit Company, New Rochelle, N.Y. Managed a truck route with complete responsibility for orders and stocking.
SUMMER 1980	**SALES CLERK** Caldor, Yonkers, N.Y. Sales and stock work with responsibility for promoting new products. Commended by department managers for assembling displays for special promotions.
SKILLS:	Programming Language: BASIC Bookkeeping and Accounting
ACTIVITIES:	Member of Gospel Singing Group Substitute Sunday School Teacher
INTERESTS:	Softball, Football, Basketball
REFERENCES:	Will be furnished on request.

Kevin M. Burk
412 Fernwood Street
Floral Park, New York 11047
(718) FL7-9872

Objective: To obtain a challenging position in the area of finance.

Education: Saint John's University, Jamaica, New York
Graduate School of Business Administration
Degree: M.B.A., August 1983
Concentration: Finance
Grade Average: 3.3 (4=A)

Manhattan College, Riverdale, New York
Degree: B.S., 6/82
Double Major: Economics and Biology

Experience: Four Corners Inn, Glen Oaks, New York
Cook and bartender; presently a 15-hour week.

1/83 Fischer's Motors, New Hyde Park, New York
Worked under the controller in improving the inventory system.

7/82-11/82 Pinewood Bar and Grill, Riverdale, New York
Bartender.

6/82 Cohen's Transport Service, Bronx, New York
Delivered U.S. mail to post offices from a distribution center before classes.

Summer 1981 Penn Central Railroad, New York, New York
Crossing watchman and track gang.

1979-1980 Nuzzi Contractors, Floral Park, New York
Summers Truck and container maintenance.

Extracurricular Resident Advisor; Varsity Soccer Captain; Fraternity
Activities: Social Chairman; Initiator of College Spring Soccer
Program, Member of Omicron Delta Kappa - national honorary society.

Background: Have lived in the New York area for over 20 years.
Interests include tennis, skiing, sailing and music.

References: Available upon request.

RESUME OF
ROBERTA BORGAN
74 Park Avenue   Bronx, New York 10455
(212) 245-4556

OBJECTIVE: To secure an entry level position where my interest in financial management can be utilized and developed.

EDUCATION: Masters in Business Administration, with Honors
Major: Financial Management
Pace University
White Plains, New York
July 1983

Bachelor of Arts
Major: Psychology
Elmira College
Elmira, New York
June 1971

EMPLOYMENT   Susan Marlowe Figure Salons
1978-1983   200 Hamilton Avenue
White Plains, New York
Assistant Manager/Exercise Instructor
Duties: Supervision of employees in the manager's absence, program
sales, conducting calisthenics classes, servicing members, planning and
coordinating promotional events, completing daily statistical reports.

1973-1977   Tompkins County Department of Social Services
108 East Green Street
Ithaca, New York
Senior Welfare Examiner
Duties: Total supervision of five welfare examiners. Hiring, consultations,
evaluations, group and individual conferences with workers, and interpret-
ing state and federal regulations for workers. Examined and authorized all
paperwork and budgets. Liaison with other social service agencies in the
community. Interviewing applicants for public assistance, documenting all
information and determining financial eligibility.

REFERENCES: On request.

GREGORY T. PHILLIPS
108-43 Homelawn Street
Jamaica, New York 11432
(718) OL 7-8843

OBJECTIVE   Challenging position in business management that will allow the opportunity to gain in the accounting and finance functions of a large company.

EDUCATION   MONROE COLLEGE, Yonkers, New York
9/82 - present   Currently enrolled in program leading to an M.B.A.

                   Concentration is in financial management with special emphasis on the study of accounting for management control.

9/78-6/82   UNIVERSITY OF FAIRFIELD, Fairfield, Connecticut

                   B.S. Major in Real Estate and Urban Economic Development. Extensive course work in real property appraisal and investment analysis.

EMPLOYMENT   MONROE COLLEGE, Yonkers, New York
9/83-10/83   Assistant to the manager of analytical studies

                   (Six-week internship). Collected synthesized price data for College's annual inflation study. Project involved library research as well as telephone contact with college suppliers. Internship led to current part-time position of coordination draft for final report.

6/81   EATON REAL ESTATE, New Canaan, Connecticut

                   Real estate salesperson. Employed part-time by Eaton for buying and selling real property.

9/80-6/82   UNIVERSITY OF FAIRFIELD, Fairfield, Connecticut

                   Head resident. Responsible for running all aspects of a college dormitory. Duties included supervising residents, kitchen and maintenance staff and preparing all paperwork for Department of Student Affairs. Job was concurrent with full-time academic study to earn seventy percent of college expenses.

SUMMERS   MONROE COLLEGE, Yonkers, New York
1980
                   Dispatcher. Employed by physical plant department with responsibility for keeping accurate records on thirty-vehicle motor pool.

1979   Groundsperson. Responsible for maintenance of college buildings and grounds.

REFERENCES   Available on request.

William Morgan
318 Market Drive
Reston, Virginia 22091
(703) 476-5528

OBJECTIVE: A position in corporate finance offering
                    challenge and responsibility

EDUCATION: B.S., Business Administration - 1983
                    Georgetown University
                    Concentration: Marketing
                    Minor: English

ACTIVITIES: Treasurer, Student Government,
                    Intramurals

EXPERIENCE: Reston Board of Education, Reston, Virginia
9/81 - 5/83   Assistant to Business Manager (part-time)
                    *Responsible for monthly bank reconciliations
                    and postings.
                    *Prepared final reports of Federal projects
                    launched in conjunction with Virginia Education
                    Department; gathered information, analyzed
                    data and authorized expenditures.

SUMMERS   Purple Cow Ice Cream Parlor
1980-1981   Alexandria, Virginia
                    Waiter/Cook

MOBILITY: Willing to relocate

REFERENCES: Provided upon request

RÉSUMÉ

Gunter Hammett

Present Address	Permanent Address
7301 Mullins Apt. #136 Houston, Texas 77081 Telephone: 713-776-8657	14 Boulder Place Yonkers, New York Telephone: 914-555-3455

JOB
OBJECTIVE

A position as an actuarial trainee in an insurance company.

EDUCATION

Rice University, Houston, Texas. Candidate for a Master in Applied Mathematical Sciences degree in May, 1983.
Concentration in probability and statistics with courses in operations research, numerical analysis, accounting as well as computer experience. Received three-quarters tuition stipend for academic year 1982-1983.

Did graduate work in philosophy at Rice University completing all departmental requirements for the M.A. degree, except the thesis. Supported by the department fellowship for academic year 1982-1983.

Received B.A. degree, cum laude, from the State University of New York at Buffalo in September 1980. Joint major in philosophy and German. Studied at the University of Wurzburg, West Germany, senior year as participant in a program sponsored by the State University of New York. Four years of college partially supported by a New York State Regents Scholarship.

WORK
EXPERIENCE

Sales clerk at Two Guys department store in Rochester, New York from October, 1980 to July, 1981. Promoted to manager trainee for area including appliances, electrical, and camera departments.

Taught German to G.I.'s at the U.S. Army installation in Wurzburg, West Germany.

Sales clerk part-time during high school at Normandie Piano and Music Center in Yonkers, New York.

PERSONAL
BACKGROUND

President of National Honor Society senior year in high school. Studied German at Goethe Institute in Arolsen, West Germany and lived with a German family while there.

ACTIVITIES

Photography, music and reading.

REFERENCES

Will be furnished upon request to the Rice University Placement Office, P.O. Box 1892, Houston, Texas 77001.

RICHARD FRANKLIN

14 Poplar Street   Minneapolis, Minnesota 55437   (612) 445-6198

Objective   Investment Analyst

Education   Rutherford State College   Rutherford, New Jersey
                        Graduate School of Business Administration
                        M.B.A., 1983

                        Seton College   Newark, New Jersey
                        B.A., 1982   Major: Economics

Experience   American Motor Credit Corporation
7/80 to present   Port Jervis, New York
                        Present finance packages (equity and lease) to
                        retail customers of truck, farm, and
                        construction equipment. Handle retail
                        collections and repossessions.

Achievements   Member, executive council Beta Beta Beta
and Interests   Honorary Society.
                        Working knowledge of Basic and Fortran.
                        Compete and officiate at track and field events.

References   Furnished upon request

HARRIS WINTERS
108 Myrtle Avenue
St. Paul, Minnesota 55149
(612) 654-8290

EDUCATION

University of Minnesota   St. Paul, Minnesota
B.B.S., June 1982
Concentration: Management
Dean's List   GPA 3.4

EXPERIENCE
Summer
1982-1983

Hy's Department Store St. Paul, MN
Part-time positions in Customer Relations
department and Personnel office.
Financed 75% of college education.

Summer
1981-1982

Meyers, Inc., Marketing Consulting Firm
Minneapolis, MN
Administrative Assistant
Coordinated activities of Vice President in
planning and research department.
Monitored office operations and projects to
insure deadlines were met.
Prepared monthly profit and loss statements
for approximately 30 clients.

Interests

Travel, tennis and skiing

References

Available upon request

NATALIE SION
22 Waller Street   Ossining, NY 10562
(914) 762-7690

CAREER
OBJECTIVE: Seeking an entry level position in the field of Management with
                 preference in Marketing.

EDUCATION: Syracuse University, Syracuse, New York
                 Bachelor of Science, May 1983
                 School of Management
                 Majors: Marketing
                           Transportation and Physical Distribution

LANGUAGES: Bilingual: English and Spanish

QUALIFICATIONS: ADMINISTRATIVE SKILLS
   - Performed analysis of accounts, invoicing of local and international
     accounts.
   - Issued payroll checks for Inca Land Tours, Cuzco.
   - Maintained journal on client contacts and services.
   - Negotiated contracts with hotels, passenger carriers, tour guides
     and other travel agencies.
   - Planned and programmed individual and group package tours.
   - Recorded and filed memberships for the Spanish Professionals
     in America.

   SUPERVISORY SKILLS
   - Assisted in setting up and organizing three travel agencies in Peru.
   - Coordinated the responsibilities of the agencies and their employees.
   - Instructed international students (elementary school) as a bilingual
     teacher assistant.

   COMMUNICATIVE SKILLS
   - Experienced customer contact as sales clerk in Dey Brothers Stores
     (Syracuse), and as tours sales representative for ILT Lima Inter-
     national.
   - Performed social and personal assistance to families and students
     enrolled in the English as a Second Language Program (Syracuse).
   - Tutored private students in Spanish and Literature.
   - Translated for the International Division at L.B. Smith Co.
   - Constant contact with patrons at the Syracuse University Mathe-
     matics Library as an assistant librarian.

WORK HISTORY:
9/79-5/83   S.U. Mathematics Library — Librarian-assistant
8/80-3/81   ALDEEU Spanish Professionals in America — Secretary
9/78-8/79   Syracuse City School District — Teacher Assistant ESL.
8/78-10/79   Dey Brothers Stores (Syracuse) — Sales Clerk
10/73-5/76   Inca Land Tours S.A. (Peru) — Promotion and International Sub-manager.

REFERENCES: Available on request.

Nancy Cohen

3 Pin Oak Lane
Chappaqua, N.Y. 10514
(914) 997-1221 Day
(914) 238-9524 Evening

PROFESSIONAL OBJECTIVE:	A challenging career in the field of <u>Marketing</u>, with opportunity to advance to executive level.
SUMMARY OF QUALIFICATIONS:	Organizational skills Ability to learn quickly Highly motivated Creative Easily adaptable to new environments
EDUCATION:	<u>Bachelor of Science in Business Administration, 1983</u> University of Hartford, Barney Business School, West Hartford, Conn. <u>Associate of Arts in Liberal Arts, 1980</u> University of Hartford, College of Basic Studies, West Hartford, Conn.
ACTIVITIES:	Social Committee, one year American Marketing Association, two years Campus Assistant (gave tours to incoming freshmen and worked at information desk), two years
WORK EXPERIENCE: (part-time & summer) 1982	<u>Salesperson</u>. The Proving Ground, West Farms Mall, Farmington, Connecticut. Sold men's clothing, helped in coordinating clothing, wrote sales, helped display merchandise, dressed mannequins, did inventories.
1981	<u>Cashier</u>. Genovese Drugs, Bloomfield, Connecticut. Sales, priced, displayed merchandise.
1981	<u>Salesperson</u>. Sym's Department Store, Elmsford, New York. Women's department. Worked in dressing room, priced and organized merchandise.
1980	<u>Receptionist/Researcher</u>. Arthur Vincent Contracting Co., Inc. Answered phone, set up interviews, researched zoning maps for land on which to build, opened and closed office.
1980	<u>Cashier/Salesperson</u>. Millwood Chemist (pharmacy), Millwood, New York. Responsible for maintaining store, displayed and priced cosmetics.
INTERESTS:	Travel, tennis, backgammon.
REFERENCES:	Available on request.

JOYCE FREELEY

ADDRESS

30 Manor Avenue
White Plains, New York 10605
(914) 948-4350

EDUCATIONAL EXPERIENCE

East Carolina University
Greenville, North Carolina
BSBA Degree Marketing Management
June 1, 1983

WORK EXPERIENCE

Travel Representative/Coordinator

Siena Travel
726 East 233rd Street
Bronx, New York 10466
May, 1982 to September, 1982
May, 1983 to Present

Sales Representative

Sisto Real Estate
728 East 233rd Street
Bronx, New York 10466
May, 1982 to September, 1982
May, 1983 to Present

Waitress

Stouffers Hotel Restaurant, Crystal City, Washington, D.C.
May, 1981 to September, 1981

Stouffers Inn of Westchester, Harrison, New York
March, 1978 to August, 1979

COLLEGE ACTIVITIES

Homecoming Committee
Special Attractions Committee
Day Student Legislator
Participated in many intramural sports while in college.

HOBBIES

Racquetball, Horseback Riding and Travel.

REFERENCES

References available on request.

LAURENCE HENRY
25 Jaylard Lane
Tucson, Arizona 85706
(602) 953-2196

Professional Objective: To obtain a marketing position in a
                          dynamic and growing company

Education: University of Arizona, Tucson, Arizona
                B.B.A. May 1983 - Cum Laude
                Major - Marketing
                Grade point average - 3.45/3.8 in major field of study
                Related course work - 15 hours of Accounting
                                      12 hours of Economics

Work Experience:
                May 1976 - Present
                ABC Electronics Corporation, Tucson, Arizona
                Bookkeeper/Sales (part-time)
                Responsible for balancing accounts receivable and
                payable as well as monthly summary sheets, general
                ledger, company payroll. Worked with company
                accountant in formulating company taxes. Participated
                in purchasing and sales of electronic components.

                December 1976 - November 1981
                Golden Bowling, Tucson, Arizona
                Assistant Manager (part-time)
                Responsible for the handling of all monies made during
                hours worked, as well as the opening and closing of
                bowling lanes. Also helped with the Saturday morning
                Junior League.

Activities and Honors:
                Dean's Honor List three semesters
                (Spring '82, Fall '80 and '81)
                Intramural basketball and football
                Member of American Bowling Congress (A.B.C.)

Comments: Willing to travel and/or relocate

References will be furnished upon request

HENRY ROBERTS
35 Franklin Road
White Plains, New York 10605
(914) 489-6103

OBJECTIVE	Seeking a professional career position in marketing that offers opportunity for dedicated corporate service as well as personal growth.
EDUCATION	Bachelor of Science, January 1983, Fordham University College of Business Administration, Bronx, N.Y.
	Major: Business Administration Concentration: Marketing
	Associate in Science, May 1980, Westchester Community College Business Administration - Management Valhalla, N.Y.
	Earned 80% of college expenses.

EXPERIENCE

6/82-12/82

White Plains Chamber of Commerce and Industry
White Plains, N.Y.
Marketing Department - Internship
- Surveyed members to assess critical business problems
- Developed Small Business Members Directory
- Provided general direction and advice to members on Chamber services
- Assisted in Chamber Corporate Relocation Project
- Participated actively in Small Business Council Meetings

6/81

Stevens Publishing Company - New York, N.Y.
Computer Operator
- Operated Tandem Model 16, Data General Eclipse 330
- Revised and maintained tape library, data logs
- Conferred with various departments pertaining to scheduling jobs
- Began as temporary employee; currently on a permanent part-time basis

Full Time
12/79 - 6/81

National Bank of Westchester - White Plains, N.Y.
Computer Operator
- Operated IBM System 3 Model 10, System 34
- Supervised in absence of shift manager

Part Time
9/79 - 12/79
- Scheduled jobs, trained new operators, performed bank reconciliation

Summer
1976-1979

Westchester Country Club - Harrison, N.Y.
Club Service Manager
- Supervised two co-workers, waited on customers in Pro Shop, caddied intermittently
- Devised system storing members' equipment, maintained golf carts and practice range

EXTRA-CURRICULAR ACTIVITIES AND INTERESTS

Marketing Society, Budget Committee, Concert Committee, Jogging, Golf, Intercollegiate and Intramural Football

REFERENCES

Available upon request.

IRENE C. NEWMEYER

HOME ADDRESS: 84-84 Dalny Road • Jamaica, New York 11432 • (718) 523-1904

SCHOOL ADDRESS: 4309 Hortensia Avenue • San Diego, California 92130 • (714) 297-9952

JOB OBJECTIVE	A position offering challenge and responsibility in consumer affairs, marketing or advertising research.
EDUCATION	THE UNIVERSITY OF CALIFORNIA
1979-1983	Graduating in May 1983 with a B.A. Degree in MARKETING AND CONSUMER BEHAVIOR. DEAN'S LIST DISTINCTION. Field of study includes: marketing and advertising theory and research, economics, business law, calculus, mass communications, statistics, psychology, sociology, and research methodology. BERKELEY COURSES: Social and Managerial Concepts in Marketing, Consumer Behavior, Product Policy, Advertising Theory and Policies, Sales Force Management, Marketing Research.

SENIOR RESEARCH SEMINARS AND PROJECTS:
- Children and Advertising
- Marketing Research — Cash vs. Credit Retail Analysis
- Portrayal of Women in Magazine Advertising (Role Model)
- Persuasive Impact of Liquor Ads in Print Media
- The Male Contraceptive Pill: Product Development and Marketing Strategies, including Advertising
- Independent study on advertising effectiveness

WORK EXPERIENCE Summers 1982	CALIFDATA CORPORATION — San Diego, California Administrative assistant in Sales Department. Trained in basic sales and organizational procedures. Responsible for record keeping, expense reports, public relations, correspondence, inventory updates, and billing.
1981	GRAHAM MILLS — La Jolla, California Basic sales and management training. Responsible for billing, orders, inventory maintenance, shipping arrangements, deliveries.
1980	THE PRESS CLUB (Office) — San Diego, California Extensive experience in inventory control, contracts, billing, correspondence and public relations.
EXTRA-CURRICULAR ACTIVITIES	Down South — responsible for soliciting advertising as well as writing copy and layout for "Intro to California." Active with Freshman Orientation Programs. UCSD Marketing and Management Club — involved with structuring innovative lecture series in career opportunities in related fields and designing community "Intern" Program. California Consumer Board — Volunteer.
REFERENCES	Available on request.

Michael Roberts
111 White Plains Road
White Plains, N.Y. 10604
(914) 948-6036

OCCUPA-TIONAL GOAL	Marketing Management
JOB OBJECTIVE	Trainee in marketing-related area such as advertising, marketing research, or public relations with the possibility of advancing to a position of more responsibility in marketing management.
EXPERIENCE	Worked an average of 30 hours a week to help pay for college.
1979-1983	MACY'S INC., White Plains, N.Y.
	Started as salesperson and was promoted to Department Sponsor. Responsibilities included scheduling lunches and breaks, authorizing exchanges and refunds, making cash deposits, setting up ads and special promotions, planning floor moves, and aiding in the taking of inventory. Managed area in manager's absence for three months. Received outstanding compliments from buyers and administrators for work done.
1976-1979	ALEXANDER'S, White Plains, N.Y.
	Salesperson in men's division. Promoted to Sunday and night supervisor after one year. Duties included scheduling breaks, setting up ads and special promotions, authorizing exchanges and refunds, training new employees, and supervising ten employees.
EDUCATION	MERCY COLLEGE
	Bachelor of Science in Business Administration with specialization in Management (May 1983) Magna Cum Laude. Cum 3.6
	HONORS
	Dean's List, four semesters
SKILLS	Foreign Language: French
	Programming Language: BASIC
ACTIVITIES	Traveling, swimming, theatre, concerts, reading, listening to music, collecting records.

Julius Martin

29 Hemlock Avenue
Dobbs Ferry, New York   10522
(914) 681-2139

Education

University of Bridgeport
B.S. 1985

Bridgeport, Connecticut
Major: Marketing
Minor: Economics

Work Experience

Travel Representative
Bluebird Travel Agency

Summers 82, 83, 84
Bridgeport, Connecticut

Assisted travel agent in booking tours, individual travel; handled
ticketing, reservations. Was responsible for all office procedure:
typing, filing, heavy phone work.

Waiter
Stouffer's

Summer 81
Harrison, N.Y.

Waited on table in 200-table restaurant; assisted in menu planning,
purchase of food, and check-in of goods; controlled inventory.

College Activities

1984   Homecoming Committee
1983   Treasurer, Debating Society
1982,83   Student Legislature

Hobbies

Swimming, horseback riding, and travel

References

Available on request

CARLA D'ANGELO
2851 Buhre Avenue
Bronx, New York   10461
(212) 823-4735

CAREER OBJECTIVE:
To obtain an entry level management position in a firm with growth potential.

EDUCATION:
FORDHAM UNIVERSITY
    Bronx, New York
    Bachelor of Science in Marketing
    Cumulative Major Index: 3.0
    September 1978 to May 1983

EMPLOYMENT HISTORY:
SAKS FIFTH AVENUE (offices)
    Yonkers, New York
    Position: Security Officer
    July 1979 to Present

    -Maintaining safety of employees
    -Protecting a National Distribution Complex
    -Training of new security officers
    -Performing internal audits
    -Producing surveillance and loss prevention reports
    -Tracing merchandise and interstore transfers via On-Line
     Cathode Ray Tube computer terminal

S.K. MERCHANDISE
    Bronx, New York
    Position: Order Clerk
    November 1978 to July 1979

    -Processed purchase orders for office supplies
    -Made appropriate adjustments to accommodate customers

GRISTEDE'S SUPERIOR FOODS
    New York, New York
    Position: Stock Clerk
    October 1976 to July 1979

    -Provided direct customer services
    -Performed various clerical duties

REFERENCES FURNISHED UPON REQUEST

LYNDA ANSBRO
29 Alan Road
White Plains, New York 10603
(914) 946-2982

OBJECTIVE:
Entry level position in the field of sales and promotion or advertising.

EDUCATION:
Mercy College, Dobbs Ferry, New York
B.B.A. Degree, Concentration in Marketing
May, 1983

RELATED
COURSEWORK:

Seminar: Women in Business	Computer: BASIC
Sales & Promotion	Advertising
Sales Function	Consumer Behavior
Management Info. Systems	Multi-National Marketing

RELATED
EXPERIENCE:

- Coordinated promotional campaign for White Plains Hospital's new perinatal building. Developed creative strategy, prepared 30-second radio commercial, utilized various types of direct mail, organized creative strategies aimed toward the recruitment of high school students for volunteer work.

- Assisted in marketing research project for Mercy College Career Development Center; gathered pertinent data and quantifiably recorded it.

- Created and conducted Management Information Systems project for Jay Products Inc., Hastings, N.Y. Identified system problems, suggested alternatives, follow-up study.

Helped finance college through the following employment:

9/77 - present:
Cashier
Finast Supermarket, White Plains, N.Y.

1975-1977:
Head Cashier
The Pizza Plaza, White Plains, N.Y.

ACTIVITIES:
American Marketing Association
Mercy College Martial Arts Club

REFERENCES:
Available upon request

Rachel Aroya
4 Ocean Road
Winthrop, Maine 04364
(207) 395-7187

OBJECTIVE   Personnel Management

EDUCATION   University of Massachusetts   Amherst, MA
                 B.S., June 1983
                 Major: Personnel Management
                 Minor: Sociology

COURSEWORK   Organizational Behavior
                 Labor Economics
                 Manpower Development
                 Employee Relations
                 Wage and Salary Administration

EMPLOYMENT   Personnel Assistant
part-time   Henry Starr Corporation Amherst, MA
9/82-6/83   Processed paper work for worker's compensation
                 cases
                 Screened and interviewed job candidates
                 Assisted with employee payroll
                 Gained exposure to EEO policies and procedures

Summers   Salesclerk
'80, '81, '82   Ralph's General Store   Winthrop, ME

LANGUAGES   Fluent in Spanish and French

REFERENCES   Provided upon request

LAURIE M. FELD • 1806 Monroe Avenue • Bronx, New York 10465 • (212) 657-0312

OBJECTIVE: A position with a firm affording the opportunity to grow to management level.

EDUCATION: PACE UNIVERSITY, Pleasantville, New York
B.B.A. Degree awarded February 1983
Major: Human Resource Management

WESTCHESTER COMMUNITY COLLEGE, Valhalla, New York
A.S. Degree awarded December 1980
Major: Business Administration

WORK EXPERIENCE: SUPEREX ELECTRONICS CORPORATION, Yonkers, New York — May 1983 to present
Administrative Assistant/National Accounts Manager. Duties include:
Compiling, reviewing and summarizing information for computer; proofreading, simplifying and
editing instruction booklet; preparing technical data for product catalogues; attending all meetings
as observer and participant; maintaining card file system on customers and product information;
correspondence and telephone contact; successful contact/interaction with different levels of
management, staff and public.

DANIEL LEE INDUSTRIES, White Plains, New York — September 1982 — March 1983
Administrative Assistant. Duties included:
Screened and interviewed applicants for potential employment; trained employees; created and
developed employment policy manuals; devised and formulated new systems for personnel
policies, employee benefits, codes for regulations and standards; expedited the work flow; kept
workload current; drew and processed checks; prepared invoices/statements and bills; handled
correspondence, telephone inquiries and other related functions.

SAVIN CORPORATION, Port Chester, New York — Summer 1982
Accounts Payable Clerk II. Duties included:
Reviewing, auditing and preparing checks for expense reports; reviewing advance requests
submitted on daily, weekly and monthly basis; working closely with the payroll department;
completing reconciliation forms to correct errors on expense reports; maintaining constant contact
with traveling employees and branch personnel with regard to expense report or reimbursement
problems.

APPAREL RETAIL CORPORATION, Boston, Massachusetts — March 1977 — February 1982
Lady's Choice — Yonkers, New York
Dimensions in Fashion — Hartsdale, New York
Assistant Manager (Day) and Night Manager. Duties included:
Supervising fifteen employees; recruiting and screening applicants for potential employment;
training employees (new and old) for various positions; training assistant managers in all phases of
the store's operations; writing employee handbook which contained rules and regulations of the
store; maintaining confidential employee personnel files; arranging daily and weekly work
schedules; computing time cards for payroll; writing up cash reports, deposits and inventory
control; dealing with public.

REFERENCES: Furnished on request.

STUART PHILLIPS

16 Court Street

Nashville, Tennessee 37028

(615) 421-6834

Career Objective: Assistant buyer in national department store

Academic History:

1982-1984   A/A Retailing

Wisconsin Junior College, Madison, Wisconsin

Honors:

1982-1984   Dean's List

Employment History:

(school year)   Martin's Department Store, Madison, Wisconsin

1982-1984   Salesperson. Designed part of purchase materials,

display, racks and exhibits. Preparation and

coordination of fashion shows.

Additional Skills: Working knowledge of fashion, illustration and

layout.

References: Available on request

Specialized Fields

ALYSON REXDALE
60 West End Avenue
New York, N.Y. 10023

(212) 866-5332

EDUCATION:

M.S., Elementary Education, Brampton College, Rochester, N.Y. 1983.

New York State Teacher's Certificate (N-6) #489664101, effective September, 1983.

B.A., Psychology. State University of New York at Albany, 1981.

EXPERIENCE:

1982-1983   Teacher, Stuyvesant Elementary School, Rochester, New York. Took into account long-range goals of individual students as well as class as a unit, and developed and organized unit in consumer education utilizing visual and audio media. Created and developed working models for use by children to promote coordination and mental stimulation.

1980-1981   Tutored German children in English while at German University in Stuttgart on Exchange Study Program.

SPECIAL RECOGNITION:

New York State Regents Scholarship - 1977-1981.

REFERENCES:

Will be furnished upon request.

```
Bertha Baker
12-20 Jeckyll Drive
Skokie, Illinois  60031                        (312) 321-3332
```

Objective   To obtain a position as an Elementary School
                   or Special Education teacher.

Certification   Elementary and Special Education, Illinois

Education   Northwestern University   Chicago, Illinois
1979-1983   B.S. in Elementary and Special Education
                   4.0 GPA
                   Dean's List

Field Experience   SPECIAL EDUCATION STUDENT TEACHING
9/82-6/83   Stephens Elementary School Chicago, Illinois
                   Developed and implemented individual education
                   plans for children. Assessed student needs.

1/81-6/81   ELEMENTARY STUDENT TEACHING
                   Hollins Avenue Elementary School
                   Chicago, Illinois
                   Instructed students individually and in
                   groups. Administered formal and informal
                   reading and math tests to diagnose individual
                   needs and levels.

Work Experience   Camp Hill and Dale   Winsted, Conn.
Summers 1981   Program Coordinator
       1980   Supervised Counselors, coordinated
                   activities.   Instructed music.

Additional Skills Piano, guitar, accordian

References   Upon request

Arnold Masters
108 Madera Court
Roswell, Georgia 30075
(404) 922-9100

OBJECTIVE   Position in the Structural and/or Geotechnical field in a Design and/or Supervisory capacity.

EDUCATION   B.E. in Civil Engineering, December 1983
                Georgia Institute of Technology — Atlanta, Georgia
                A.A.S. in Civil Technology, May 1980
                Southern Technological Institute — Marietta, Georgia
                Financed 50% of college education.

EXPERIENCE   1980 - Present - Schoor Associates, Atlanta, Georgia.
                Diversified free-lance engineering services.
                Responsibilities include energy surveys for implementation of energy management systems,
                design of high rise and computer facilities, fire detection and prevention systems. Drafting
                services for private consulting firms in the mechanical, electrical and plumbing fields.

                1977 - 1980 - Carpentry work done privately for real estate firms and commercial
                projects in Atlanta area.

HONORARY &   Chi Epsilon (Civil Engineering Honor Society).
PROFESSIONAL   First Honors Deans List; ranked in top 25% of graduating class. Member A.S.C.E.
ACTIVITIES

MISCEL-
LANEOUS   Speak and write Portuguese fluently and have a working knowledge of Spanish. Available for
                travel and relocation.

REFERENCES: Available on request.

JUDITH COLEMAN
38 WASHINGTON AVENUE   BETHEL, CONNECTICUT 06804
(203) 744-5901

EDUCATION

B.S. University of Connecticut, Storrs, CT
Hotel, Restaurant, and Travel Administration
May 1982

WORK
EXPERIENCE

CAMP BELAIR, Amherst, MA
Assistant Food Service Director
- supervised staff of three workers
- controlled inventories
- purchased food and checked in goods
- developed menus and marketed new items
- prepared a variety of foods served
- controlled cash inflow and outflow
- supervised special catering functions
- voluntarily assisted in other camp functions
Summer 1981, 1980

THE HARTFORD PLAZA, Hartford, CT
Front Office Cashier
- trained and supervised new employees
- handled all general queries of public
- prepared pre-audit reports
- directed day-to-day activities for hotel guests
  (billing, checking out, traffic at front desk)
September 1979 — September 1981 (part-time)

UNIVERSITY OF CONNECTICUT, Storrs, CT
Dining Hall Worker
September 1978 — May 1981

ACTIVITIES

International Food Service Executive Assoc. Student Chapter
HRTA Career Day Hostess, March 1979
New York Hotel Show Hostess
Residence Hall Council
Campus Fire Chief

SKILLS

BASIC Computer Programming

CERTIFICATION

Standard First Aid to the Injured

REFERENCES

Available on request

PAUL MARKS
3519 Palisades Avenue
Riverdale, New York 10463
(212) 549-2080

EDUCATION:

EMORY UNIVERSITY LAW SCHOOL
Atlanta, Georgia JD 1984
  Graduated in top 15% of class
  Dean's List 1981, 1982
  Recipient American Jurisprudence
  Award, Conflicts, 1982

YALE UNIVERSITY
New Haven, Conn. BA 1980
  Graduated in three years with
  honors

BAR ADMISSION:

NEW YORK STATE BAR to be taken
September 1984

LEGAL EMPLOYMENT:

Present

Assistant District Attorney
Office of the District Attorney
New York County
  Responsible for the preparation
  and litigation of felony cases
  in the Supreme Court
  Drafted and argued various
  motions related thereto
  Drafted appeals to the Supreme
  Court, Appellate Division,
  First Department

1983-1984

Legal Intern, Office of the
United States Attorney
Atlanta, Georgia
  Drafted motions and assisted
  in the preparation of cases
  for trial

1983 (Summer):

Department of Health, Education,
and Welfare
Atlanta, Georgia
  Drafted responses to appeals
  taken from administrative
  hearings on disability benefits

REFERENCES:

Available upon request

Mario Charlestian
12 Meadowbrook Drive
Philadelphia, Pa. 19012   (215) 614-1436

Objective: An entry-level position in community services.

Education:

1985   MSW   University of Pennsylvania, Philadelphia, Pa.
1983   BA   Barnard College, New York, N.Y.

Experience:

Summers   COUNSELOR/ASSISTANT CASEWORKER
'84 &'85   Child Home Services, Philadelphia, Pa.
              Held initial interview with prospective parents
              for adoption processes. Did preliminary review
              and prepared evaluations. Conducted follow-up
              checks and assembled data for final reports.

Summers   RESERVATIONIST
'82 &'83   United Airlines, Philadelphia, Pa.
              Performed all reservation duties; heavy phone contact
              with travel agents and the public; arranged connecting
              flights. Type and teletype; operated small computer.

Extracurricular
activity:

1983   Class President

References: Available on request.

ETHEL ADLER
98 Longwood Drive
Phoenix, Arizona 85073
(602) 442-1151

OBJECTIVE   Dietician

EDUCATION   B.S., Michigan State University 1982
                   Major: Nutrition
                   Minor: Chemistry
                   Dean's List throughout four years of college

                   Emphasis of study was on commercial food
                   processing; specialization in food for the
                   elderly.

EXPERIENCE   Assistant Dietician (part-time), Food
1982-Present   Service Department, Masonic Temple, Detroit,
                   Michigan
                   Planned menus and supervised preparation of
                   all meals.

Summers   Assistant to Chief Dietician, Marlboro State
1979-1981   Hospital; Marlboro, Michigan
                   Helped translate convalescent diets into
                   actual meals. Selected and delivered
                   special meals to diet patients

INTERESTS   Gourmet cooking, camping, hiking

REFERENCES   Furnished upon request

PAMELA SUMMERS
46 OCEAN PARKWAY   LOS ANGELES, CALIFORNIA 10623
(213) 619-4628

EDUCATION:
1985   University of California, Berkley, California
                       B.S. Nursing
                       3.6 out of 4.0

Honors   Phi Beta Kappa   Graduated Magna Cum Laude

WORK
EXPERIENCE:
Summer   LABORATORY ASSISTANT
1984   *Los Angeles General Hospital,* Los Angeles, California
                       Assisted in keying reports and preparing slides for testing.
                       Kept records of daily tests, miscellaneous research. Cleaned
                       and checked equipment.

Summer   KEYPUNCH OPERATOR
1983   *Jameson Medical Industries,* Los Angeles, California
                       Worked under the direction of the Group Head transcribing data from source
                       documents to punch cards. Operated alphabetical and numerical key
                       punch and key reviews. Located on the source document items to be punched.
                       Served as relief receptionist.

Summer   FILE CLERK
1982   *First National Bank,* Los Angeles, California
                       Arranged, sorted, and filed invoices, reports, and correspondence. Retrieved
                       and filed items as requested. Responsible for miscellaneous typing
                       assignments.

LANGUAGES: Fluent Spanish

HOBBIES: Reading, cooking, swimming

REFERENCES: Available on request.

The Job Search

Your job search begins in your own backyard! Of all the various job sources, the most convenient—and at times the best—are your friends, relations, and neighbors. Everyone you know, including your doctor, dentist, former Scout leader, den mother, or father might be the very person to furnish you with the lead you've been looking for. So, when looking for a job, don't keep it a secret. The philosophy of your campaign is to let as many people as possible know that you are job hunting.

Don't be secretive or embarrassed about asking for help. Enlist the support of as many people as you possibly can. People like to help. Turn the situation around; if you were working and a friend or acquaintance asked you for help, wouldn't you be eager to assist in any way you could?

Everyone has looked for a job at one time or another and therefore, is able to identify and become very empathetic toward a person looking for a job—especially when it's the very first after graduation. Don't be shy and, whenever possible, give the person you've spoken to a copy or copies of your résumé. You might be very surprised to know how fast résumés get circulated.

Often companies have policies of posting new job openings on the company bulletin board before the jobs are advertised or listed with employment agencies. The reason for this is companies *really* do want to promote from within (no outside person is interviewed for the new opening unless no one on staff either wants the job and is qualified for it) and companies prefer to hire someone recommended by an employee rather than a complete stranger.

Classified Ads

Read the ads! Not only on Sunday, but every day! Not only is there a good chance of your finding the very job of your dreams, but there is a wealth of information about the job market in your part of the country.

College grads often make the mistake of only reading the listing under "college grads" or "trainee" and are discouraged to find few, if any listings.

When searching the ads, consider every job title from A through Z. A perfect job may be listed under Administrative Assistant, Gal/Guy Friday, Secretary, Research Assistant, Paralegal Assistant, Public Relations Assistant, Assistant Editor, Editorial Assistant, Salesperson, Publisher's Assistant, etc. A Comptroller's Assistant might very well be a Management Trainee and Secretary in advertising very possibly requires no steno and, in essence, is an opportunity to learn to be a copy writer. Be sure to read not only the job title but the copy describing the position and the qualifications required.

If you find an ad that interests you and you have *some*, but not all the requirements, it's worth investigating. More often than not, jobs are filled by people who can do the job, but don't possess all the requirements listed by the company. When a company decides to add to its staff, they will prepare the job specs for the ideal candidate. As time goes by, it becomes more and more important to fill that job. They are not, however, getting the response to the ad they expected.

The employer then realizes his or her ad was not realistic and personnel is ready to drop some of the specs and just find someone who can do the job. The same applies to salaries—a job may be listed for $15,000 and ultimately be filled for $20,000.

Since you are looking for the best job possible, it is advisable to explore as many opportunities as feasible. Go out on as many interviews as you can to learn as much as you can about each job offered. Then, after careful consideration of each job together with all its benefits, opportunities and ramifications, you accept the one which most closely resembles what you are looking for.

When answering ads be sure to follow specific directions for each particular ad. If a phone number is listed, you'd be correct in inferring they would like you to call and set up an appointment. Do so. Don't arrive without warning. You might think it shows enthusiasm, it doesn't. It shows a lack of concern and can only waste your time, the interviewer's time and create unnecessary hostility.

If a box number is listed, reply by sending your résumé with a covering letter. (Covering letters will be discussed in Chapter 7.)

Don't be discouraged if you don't get immediate results. At times, as much as three months elapse before receiving a response from your résumé. This is par for the course!

Remember, job hunting is harder, more traumatic, and more frustrating than working, but once you find a job the weeks or months of anxiety will be forgotten immediately.

While studying the want ads, you can measure how realistic you are in terms of existing jobs. Look closely at the salaries offered for recent college graduates. Is your minimum in line? If not, do a little thinking and bring your expectations closer to reality.

Are you one of the many college graduates who is "philosophically" opposed to typing, although you find many of the most interesting job listings require typing? If so, I am very sympathetic, and am aware that no one goes to college to become a typist, but to absolutely refuse to use your typing, or if you are determined not to a acquire such a marketable skill, you are doing yourself a tremendous disservice.

Companies are well aware that a college graduate will not be happy in either a clerk-typist or straight typist job, and they realize that an unhappy employee, in all probability, will not work out. Employers are, without exception, very cost conscious. Hiring and "breaking in" a new employee is an expensive process for a company. In addition to the clerical costs of setting up a new personnel file, adding to the insurance roster, setting up payroll cards, etc., there is also the fact that many offices feel that few employees can actually *earn* their salaries until having worked for that employer for at least three months. One of the functions of the personnel department, department heads, and anyone involved in recruiting is the avoidance of any kind of expense by making very sure that the job specifications are correct—and the mistake of hiring candidates that are either "underqualified" or "over qualified" does not occur.

It is difficult for a recent graduate to distinguish between those jobs requiring typing that are actually dead ends and those jobs that offer an opportunity for growth and advancement. What is further complicating, interviewers don't like to make absolute promises of just where a job will lead. Though an interviewer can learn a great deal about you from meeting you and studying your résumé, he or she still doesn't have enough information to give you a positive guarantee that in six months you'll be doing "whatever." Only time will tell how stable you are. Will you usually be prompt? Will you be absent more than would be predictable? How well will you get along with your staff? Are you as reliable as you appear? Until that is known, there can be no promises.

Fortunately, the decision as to whether or not a particular job has potential is actually not as esoteric as I may have implied. Remember, the interviewer's job is to hire the very best person he or she can possibly find who will be an asset, not only in the short term, but in the long-term employment. The interviewer is trained to *know* that college grads are looking for a job with potential; so if you receive an offer you can be sure the job has career possibilities and will offer much responsibility and opportunity for advancement.

While browsing through the classified ads make special note to study all information pertaining to employment agencies. You may find many employment agencies run "institutional ads" usually close to the beginning of the sections of the want ads or classifieds. The institutional ads give the name and address of the agency and a representative listing of jobs they are trying to fill. Studying these ads closely will help you decide which of these agencies might be helpful to you. The agency advertisements might make note of its specialty; if not, you can tell by the nature of the sample job listings. Any employment agency listing one vice-president position after another, exclusively, is very unlikely to be interested in interviewing a recent college graduate. You can safely exclude such an agency from your search.

Skim through the classified ads and look for spot ads with the name and address of an employment agency. By law, any employment agency must include the word *agency* in its name. You can tell by the nature of the ads whether a specific agency may be helpful to you. If you find an agency that advertises one job that you think you might qualify for, by all means make a point of registering with that agency as quickly as possible. If, on the other hand, you find an agency that doesn't list any job you specifically qualify for, but does carry some advertisements that might appeal to you, it would be worth while to visit that agency also.

Employment Agencies

No job search can be considered complete without the help of the *appropriate* private employment agency. By appropriate, I mean an agency that is geared toward placing recent college graduates. Obviously, an agency whose expertise lies in the area of the recruitment of Certified Public Accountants and Comptrollers would not be right for you.

You can find some valuable information right in your local classified newspaper ads.

Of course, the ideal way of finding the agency best suited to your needs is personal recommendations. Don't be afraid to ask anyone you know (working or searching like yourself) if they would be willing to give you some suggestions. You'll be surprised at not only how cooperative they will be in giving you this information, but how many will go one step further and suggest you use their name. Little by little, your job sources or contact list will grow larger.

It's an excellent idea to call personnel departments of some of the companies you would like to work for, and, after explaining that you're a recent graduate, ask if they could possibly recommend a suitable employment agency.

I'm sure you will not only receive many excellent suggestions, but a few of the companies you called asking for advice will invite you to meet a staff member for an interview.

When you get to the agency, make sure to follow their rules. If they ask you to call to make an appointment, by all means do so; if the agency has special interviewing hours, be sure to visit during those hours; if they ask you to fill out an application *even though you have a résumé*, do so (there are some very valid reasons for this, by the way!). Don't balk, complain, or question. *Simply cooperate.*

A private employment agency has just one source of income—that is earning fees by getting people jobs. Therefore, an agency has more than a casual interest in helping you to find a job, and, if used correctly, can become a powerful ally in your search. Registering with an agency is equivalent to applying for a number and a variety of jobs.

Your counselor will want to know what kind of job you are interested in and what your salary minimum is. He or she will be a good judge of whether your aspirations are realistic and might suggest certain compromises. Listen with an open mind. Counselors are very much in touch with employers' needs and have a finger on the pulse of the job market.

After establishing rapport, your placement counselor or manager (as they are often called) will describe those openings which he or she feels will both interest you and for which you are qualified. You are under no obligation to go to *all* or *any* of those jobs suggested. You make the choice and the counselor will make the referral to only those positions.

Go on as many interviews as you possibly can. I've had so much experience in referring college grads to a mediocre-sounding job with a good company and being pleasantly surprised at the outcome. The applicant would go with the feeling that, though the job didn't sound that special, they would benefit from the experience of being interviewed and if they created a good impression, they might be considered for a job opening sometime in the future. The candidates were pleased and surprised to find the interview resulted in a job offer—not the one they were referred to but a much more interesting position which had just become available.

If, after the first interview with the agency, none of the jobs described is suitable, you will be kept on file and considered for every new opening that arises. Effectively, the agency does the legwork for you and will keep you informed of each new position. Most agencies expect and need several copies of your résumé, and you should be prepared to supply them.

Some counselors like their applicants to call once a week to "check in" to see if anything has developed; others prefer *not* to be called—*they* will call when they have something to discuss. It's a good idea to ask your counselor if he or she prefers to be called and, if so, how often.

Agencies charge a fee for their services. This fee is usually paid by the employer, but it may be paid by the employee (only in the event that the agency finds you a job that you have willingly accepted), or the fee may be reimbursed by the employer. That means the applicant will pay the fee if the agency's referral results in both a job offer and an acceptance. Usually the fee is expected to be paid in six installments, and after either three months, six months, or one year, the employer reimburses the fee to its new employee. Whatever the arrangements, it is imperative that you completely understand the terms. It is important that you read the contract, if there is one, and answer any questions regarding your obligation before you sign the contract.

As with any business arrangement, it is of utmost importance that you have a clear understanding of your legal obligation at the beginning of the relationship.

Don't be surprised if you are *not* asked to sign a contract. Many agencies that work *only* on positions where the employer pays the fee, don't expect their applicants to sign any contract.

State Employment Agencies

No matter what part of the country you are living in, I am sure it is possible for you to register with the United States Employment Service or one of its affiliates. The state agencies operate over 2,500 local offices to serve persons seeking employment and employers trying to recruit new employees. The services of the state agencies are very similar to those of the private agencies, with the exception that the government agencies charge no fee, either to the employer or the job applicant. Their functions are supported by the government.

Every serious job seeker should visit the local government employment office. They very often are a fine source of job leads. Like private employment agencies, the counselors at the state employment offices are very knowledgeable about government jobs, and they will be glad to share this information with you. They will be very glad to answer any questions about market conditions in your area, available government jobs, or anything you feel would help you in your job search.

Government Jobs

Though at the moment there is a lot of talk about layoffs in government jobs (essentially no more than layoffs in private industry) there are still tremendous opportunities for those who join forces with the government and become one of its employees. As the economy improves, the government will continue to recruit and, in all probability, will remain the largest employer in the country. The U.S. Government employs over 17 million Americans. One out of every six employed people serve either federal, state, or local governments. The federal government employs 2.8 million, state governments employ 4 million, and local government agencies employ over 8 million. U.S. government agencies hire 13,000–18,000 recent college graduates a year. These figures represent a very significant percentage of our work force and, therefore, every job seeker should seriously consider a government job.

The range of job offerings is staggering. Doctors, dentists, veterinarians, attorneys, secretaries, and clerks are hired by the government, as well as pilots, teachers, economists, engineers, gardeners, and chauffeurs. Think of any job classification, and you can safely bet the government hires people in that category.

Almost anyone employed by the government will tell you that they are the recipient of the best benefits: government jobs offer the most security (even in this recent recession, the government *did not* lay off as large a percentage of employees as industry), the most superior health plans, the most liberal vacations, and the most extensive retirement plans.

The government depends heavily on testing. Certain educational and experience requirements must be met in order to *apply* for a specific job. Only if you have the necessary requirements will you be entitled to take the examination for the job. The exam is both determinative and competitive. That is, you must achieve a certain grade in order to be eligible for the job, but the job will be offered first to the person achieving the highest score on the test. Depending upon what test a candidate might be applying for, the test may be written, practical, or physical.

Obviously different strengths must be measured if one is being tested for a state police officer or a laboratory assistant. Should you take the test for a government job and not score high enough (for the one you are tested for) or for any of the immediate openings, you may be eligible for a job that will open in the future.

If you are interested in government employment, be prepared for a very methodical search in seeking it out.

Unfortunately, there is *no single* office that takes care of federal, state, county, and municipal employment; each has to be applied for in its appropriate office.

For Municipal Employment Call your city or town hall and you will be told where to go and whom to see.

County Employment Call your county center (listed in your local phone book) and you will be given the appropriate information.

State Government Check the phone book to see if there is an office of the State Civil Service Commission (or Personnel Board). If not, write to the State Civil Service Commission requesting a list of current examinations and job openings. You should also request a list of current job openings and examinations and ask to be put on their regular list as you will then obtain certain up-to-date information.

Federal Civil Service The main post office in your town will have some information on openings and examinations in the Federal Civil Service.

However, to get more complete information about Federal Civil Service jobs, you should write to the main office in Washington, D.C. Request that you be put on their regular mailing list. Many people are unaware that government jobs are available abroad as well as within the United States.

Government jobs have much to offer and, if you are interested, stay with it. Read all the literature available; your local library is a fine source. Take all the tests for which you are eligible. Barron's publishes several books which are a *must* for anyone interested in a government career. I highly recommend Barron's *How to Prepare for Civil Service Examinations*.

Similar to anything else worthwhile, to "land" a government job takes tremendous perseverance but the rewards and opportunities which will become yours will surely make the effort absolutely worthwhile.

College Placement Bureaus

Very few college graduates really make full use of their placement bureaus. The average graduate visits it once, has a brief chat with the director, goes out on any interviews suggested (if there *is* an interview suggested), and waits to hear about any positions which might become available. They assume if they haven't heard from the bureau, it simply means that there are no new job openings. They expect to be called about each new opening.

Ideally, that's how it should work. But placement bureaus, like everything else, are run by people who are not infallible. It is very likely your application card has been misplaced or possibly the interviewer thought that you had gotten a job and your records were placed in the inactive file.

It is very appropriate if you haven't heard from your placement bureau to make another visit, bring more résumés, and spend enough time with the interviewer to make sure he or she remembers you. Don't be afraid to seem aggressive; remember, aggressiveness is an important personality trait when looking for a job.

Temporary Services

It seems paradoxical to suggest to job seekers looking for a *permanent* job that they should consider the possibility of working as a "temp." This is often the fastest method of getting an offer for a permanent position. Although services supplying temporary workers do not consider themselves purveyors of jobs, their serendipitous rate of placement is high.

If you consider the dynamics of the temporary industry it is easy to see the logic of this. Very often employers "rent" a temporary when there is a project that must get done and, for whatever reasons, their staff cannot finish it in the assigned time. Usually this happens when the company is understaffed, and it is not until this time that they are aware they need additional personnel.

As soon as the "temp" has covered and the work flow continues, the company becomes involved in recruiting a new employee. Quite often, our agency has found that while our permanent division is screening for a specific job, our temporary division has sent a "temp" to cover the position until it is filled. We have become accustomed to learning that the "temp" was hired on a permanent basis.

It makes sense. While the temps are often hired to provide extra work force during an occasional surge in a company's load or to fill in for a sick or vacationing employee, they are also called in to keep the work from piling up on a desk that has unexpectedly become vacant. While the original intention is to interview other people to fill the job, the temp is on the spot, becoming a person the staff know (rather than just another candidate), and has demonstrated a capability for getting the job done. It is always a good idea when going out as a "temp" to bring several résumés, and let it be known that you are looking for a permanent job.

One of our clients, a prestigious book publisher, asked us to recruit a picture researcher. The qualifications were very rigid: recent college graduate, art history major, American history minor, who could type 60 words per minute, and had at least two summers of office experience. While we were trying to find an applicant who matched these qualifications, our temporary division referred a "temp" to fill in. She had just graduated from a state college with a sociology major and history minor. Her typing was only 50 words per minute (our counselor explained to the client that since she knew the touch system and her typing was extremely accurate, her speed would pick up quickly). She was bright, cooperative, and could easily handle the assignment. While our permanent division was busy trying to find an art history major with the other qualifications, the client realized that her "temp" could handle the position better than anyone (with the absolute qualifications) she had interviewed. The sociology major was offered the job at a higher salary than she was making as a "temp." We've seen temporary figure clerks offered positions as media trainees. We've seen typists become research associates, gal/guy Fridays turn into account executive trainees. We've seen a file clerk become a social secretary to an ambassador. It takes imagination, guts, and a willingness to consider each temporary assignment an adventure.

On any temporary assignment, always make a point of working just a little harder. Try to come up with new and more efficient ways of handling some of the routine clerical work. Always be sure to have plenty of copies of your résumé with you; these people are people with contacts and most are eager to be helpful.

Temporary services can be especially advantageous to beginners or to persons who are not yet sure where their interests lie. Temporary work lets you experiment by spending a few days in one industry, perhaps a week or two in an art gallery, a month in publishing, and then a stint in a brokerage firm. It is a unique way of seeing how various fields work from the inside, while helping you to collect information for a wise and considered career choice.

Working on a temporary assignment brings no guarantee of a permanent job offer, but there is a guarantee that you'll meet a variety of people, be exposed to many different kinds of businesses, and experience myriad distinctive working conditions. Most of all, you'll be getting what every job seeker needs most—experience while getting paid for it! By all means, consider temporary work as another source on your quest for a permanent job.

Executing a well-planned direct mail campaign allows you to take control of your job campaign. Your situation changes from *passively* sending your résumé to any lead advertised to *actively* deciding whom you want your future employer to be, and then setting the wheels in motion for that to become an actuality.

The first thing you must do is compile the list of companies you would want to be employed by. In other words, target who will receive the letter and delete any organization that for one reason or another doesn't interest you.

Bear in mind that each of these companies will be sent an individually typed cover letter along with your résumé. As an entry-level college graduate, your mailing should be sent to the personnel manager of the company. The spelling of his or her name as well as the spelling of the company name must be absolutely accurate—otherwise, it will be discarded.

Fortunately, all of this information is available in the reference room of your local library and your librarian is bound to be helpful. Usually reference books cannot be taken from the library but you will be completely welcome to spend as much time as necessary to prepare a proper list.

Your field of interest will determine and will contain the information appropriate for you.

If you are interested in:	*Directory:*
General Business	Standard & Poor's
Publishing	Literary Market Place
Advertising	Standard Rate and Data
Banking and Finance	Moody's Banking and Finance Manual
	Rand McNally International Banking Manual
Law	Martindale Hubbell Directory

Copy all the information correctly—person in charge of personnel, name of personnel manager, name and address of company, zipcode. In all probability, the personnel manager's name will be listed in the directory, but if not, if you are in the same city you can simply call the company and ask for the name and spelling of his or her name. If the company is out of town, and it is impossible to get the name of the personnel manager, you can address it to Personnel Director.

The list should not be too long. You don't want to involve yourself in an interminable project that becomes so overwhelming you give up in frustration. If you are willing to relocate, do not hesitate to write to companies at a distance from your home. Most companies when faced by a really "hot" candidate will pay for the applicant's trip to their main office. As we said before, if you are willing to relocate, it should be stated on your résumé.

Your covering letter should be brief and written in a conversational tone; avoid being pompous or "cute."

It should be set up in the usual business form and each letter must be individually typed. It should never be longer than one page and should contain three or four short paragraphs. You may reproduce your résumé but never your covering letter. The letter should be centered correctly with sufficient margins all around to present an attractive appearance.

Start by saying you are enclosing your résumé and would like to be considered for any entry-level position with that company. (This information concludes paragraph 1.)

Paragraph 2 should include a short statement indicating why you feel your qualifications should interest the company and why you would like to be employed by them. If possible, refer to something in your résumé that will be of interest to your reader. You might point out some appropriate information in your educational history (perhaps your major or minor) or in your summer experience. You could mention the one summer you spent as a Friday in a public relations firm. If you're sending your résumé to a group of organizations involved with journalism, you might elaborate on this job and mention you wrote press releases, worked on feature stories, assisted in speech writing, and so on.

Your third and final paragraph should state that you'll call in a few days to arrange for an interview. *Don't wait for them to call!* As we've said before, you become the active member when you're conducting your direct mail campaign—there are certain shots you can call. Remember, the closer you get to actual personal contact, the closer you get to a job offer.

Don't be surprised if you find your direct mail campaign becomes more expensive than you anticipated. It is true that direct mail involves the cost of reproduction of résumés, stationery, a typist (if you yourself can't type well enough to create an error-free, professional-looking letter), envelopes, phone calls, postage—and time. But every other method involves as much, if not more, time. Think of times spent pounding the pavement, and the countless hours waiting in reception rooms for an interview. The very dynamics of making the rounds in a job search include the expenses for carfare, lunches, phone calls, and the inevitable, continual cups of coffee. The job hunt will cost a certain amount of money; but the investment is minimal when you consider the rewards include not only the start of a lifetime career but a guaranteed salary that will allow you to become a mature, independent person.

The Covering Letter

It's important to know how to write an attention-getting letter. Though job hunters, in general, are very aware of the vital role a well-executed résumé plays in their job campaign, few realize the importance of the covering letter.

A covering letter should be included every time you send out your résumé to a prospective employer or to anybody involved in helping you find a job. While your résumé contains all the information about your education, experience, skills, and special talents, the covering letter is not only an indication of courtesy and professional approach to job hunting, but tells *why* you are sending your résumé to that particular person.

The person who receives your résumé may be recruiting for a number of openings, each requiring a different level of experience, education, and abilities. Without the covering letter to tell *why* you sent your résumé and *what* kind of job you feel you are qualified for, you are basically asking the reader to spend extra time reading your résumé and from it *inferring* where you might be of interest to the employer. Since everyone is pressed for time and résumés arrive by the hundreds, the probability is that those résumés sent without covering letters are simply discarded.

Whether you are sending your résumé to answer a company ad, box number, employment agency, at the suggestion of a friend, or as part of your personal direct mail campaign, the covering letter will always follow the same simple rules.

1. It should be brief—never more than one page.
2. It should be addressed to a particular individual in the company, perferably by name. If you cannot ascertain the name, the letter should be addressed to the Personnel Director.
3. It should consist of two or three paragraphs.
4. It should be individually typed; unlike your résumé, it *must never be reproduced.*
5. You should use quality stationery; personal stationery is always appropriate.
6. It should be laid out typographically so it is balanced on the page and should conform to the standards of business correspondence.

The first paragraph of the covering letter should tell why you are writing to that particular company. If it is in answer to an ad , say so, and include the name and date of the publication where the ad appeared.

If you are writing at the suggestion of another person, be sure to name and identify the person who has made the suggestion. If the person was one of your professors at college, include this information. If he or she was someone who interviewed you at another company, be sure to include the name of *that* company and his or her job title. If that person is an employee of the company you are writing to, be sure to give the name, job title, or category where employed.

As we mentioned earlier, if the letter is part of your own direct mail campaign, you should explain in two or three lines why that particular company interests you.

The following one or two paragraphs should point out the features of your résumé that could be of interest to your correspondent. Since you have just graduated from college, your education, part-time experiences, and enthusiasm are your most marketable assets and you should be proud to refer to them. Possibly, one of your extracurricular activities could demonstrate a special ability that might be of interest to the potential employer.

The closing paragraph should indicate that you hope you have created enough interest in yourself to warrant an interview and are looking forward to further correspondence to arrange a meeting.

As your covering letter is used to highlight certain aspects of your résumé, the same résumé may be used to pursue different job opportunities in various fields. The covering letter, stressing your most appropriate skills, interests, and talents, can be geared to each particular company that will be the recipient of your résumé. By calling attention to a unique qualification in your résumé, it not only *strengthens* your résumé, but it *personalizes* your letter and résumé and makes it apparent that you are not simply sending out form letters to accompany your résumé.

Though enclosing a covering letter requires considerable effort, the time spent is a valid investment and will greatly increase the attention your résumé receives, and you will be pleased with the ultimate results.

Sample #1 — Reply to an Advertisement with a Box Number

16 Terrace Avenue
Chicago, IL 11625
May 3, 1983

Box Y4729
Elmira Post
189 Post Street
Elmira, NY 10629

Dear Sir:

I am replying to your advertisement in Tuesday's (May 1, 1983) *Elmira Post* for a media trainee in an advertising agency.

Your ad specified some background in economics and statistics. As you can see from my enclosed résumé, I majored in Economics and minored in Statistics, maintaining a 3.0 average. My three years of summer experience includes two summers (1981 and 1982) with Bond & Lord, a large ad agency, where I was employed as a Friday in the production department.

In my junior and senior year I was the Advertising Manager of our college newspaper and there gained some actual media experience. I hope this establishes my credentials as qualified for your opening.

If my background seems to fit your needs, please contact me at your convenience.

Your consideration is greatly appreciated.

Yours truly,

Marvin Ernest

Sample #2 — Reply to Advertisement

25 Hudson Street
Cleveland, OH 40612
May 29, 1983

Mr. Frank Ash
Personnel Manager
W. W. Hold & Company
38 West 44th Street
New York, NY 10036

Dear Mr. Ash:

I am replying to your advertisement in Sunday's (May 28, 1983) *Plain Dealer* for a Gal Friday.

As you can see from my résumé, I have just graduated from Cornell University with a major in English. Though my long-range goals are in the area of copy editing or editorial, I am realistic about the nature of entry-level jobs in publishing and feel my background may be of interest to you. I type 75 wpm, take shorthand (my own system), have used the dictaphone, and have had three summers of secretarial experience with a manufacturing company in Cleveland. I have handled my own correspondence and, unlike many other college graduates, enjoy secretarial work.

I plan to be in New York City next week, and will call you in hope of setting up an interview.

Looking forward to meeting you.

Cordially,

Susan Dean

Sample #3 — Through Personal Contact

95 Valentine Lane
Mellville, NY 10901
June 8, 1983

Ms. Jane Raymond
Personnel Director
North Bank of America
White Plains, NY 10603

Dear Ms. Raymond:

Mr. John Smith, an executive in your Manhattan office, who is a friend of my father, suggested I write to you about the possibility of an opening in your international department.

As you can see from my résumé, I am a French major and Spanish minor and am very interested in a position where I can use my knowledge of languages. I have worked as an office temporary for the past three summers and some of my assignments were in the banking field. I am a good typist (70 wpm) and would be quite willing to start in a clerical capacity.

I would like very much to meet you and am available for an interview any time convenient to you.

Sincerely yours,

John Osterio

Sample #4 — Direct Mail Campaign

36 Garrity Drive
Chicago, IL 60625
April 18, 1984

Ms. Margaret Chapman
Personnel Manager
Continental Electric
Xenobia, Maine 10874

Dear Ms. Chapman:

I am writing to you today in the hope you might read my résumé and consider me for an entry-level sales position with your company.

I was very interested in the article about your company which appeared in the New York *Times Magazine* of April 1, 1984. Your paternalistic policy which involved a "no turn-over" company complies with both my long- and short-range goals, as I am really interested in a stable opportunity.

As you can see from my résumé, I am a Psychology Major and was President of our debating society in my senior year. I feel both would indicate a talent for Sales. I did some selling in my summer job in 1982 (Capital Books) and not only was I successful in sales, but thoroughly enjoyed it.

I expect to be in your neighborhood the first week in May. I will call so that we can set up an interview at that time in the hope I can impress you as much as your company impressed me.

Your consideration is greatly appreciated.

Sincerely yours,

Richard Francis

The Interview

The interview has been set up. Finally all the hard work of your job campaign has paid off: you have been granted an interview. You have interested someone enough that he or she wants to see you. You know the time, the place; suddenly you have an attack of nerves. You're both eager and anxious. You feel that everything you did in your job campaign will be wasted if you can't connect the interview with a solid job offer.

How will it go? Will you be able to convince the interviewer that not only can you do the job, but, indeed, you are absolutely the best person they can find? All of a sudden you are not so sure you can do the job and certainly don't feel you are absolutely the best person they can find. What is happening to you happens to almost every single job hunter—you're experiencing a slight case of jitters.

If you find this happening to you, don't worry. You're in good company. Whether one is interviewing for his or her first job or is 90 percent up the corporate ladder, putting oneself in the proverbial "hot seat" can be an unsettling experience. Our experience as well as that of our colleagues all over the country confirms that the great majority of job seekers find the interview one of the most stressful experiences they have encountered.

There are ways, however, of lessening the stress of the interview. The first step is to view the interview realistically. Unfortunately, most job candidates experience the interview as an acid test of his or her abilities and self-worth. Such an attitude is extremely anxiety-producing and is bound to draw a negative response from the interviewer.

If, however, you view the interview realistically, simply as two adult *equals* getting acquainted to explore the possibility of what each has to offer the other, it can be a positive, rewarding experience. Keep in mind you and the interviewer are trying to find out if there's any way you can be beneficial to each other. Remember, always, the interview is bilateral.

The employer interviewing you is just as interested in selling the job to you as you are in selling yourself to the employer. The interviewer's job is not only to screen many applicants, but to choose the one most qualified, make a job offer, and have that offer *accepted*. Just as you are in competition with many recent graduates, the companies recruiting are similarly competing with *every* other company to hire just the right person, and the interviewer is under pressure to have the candidate who is offered the job, accept it. Don't be surprised if after a few questions about your abilities and goals, you suddenly find the interviewer is no longer asking questions about you, but is telling you of the tremendous advantages of working for that company and the unusual potential of the job now open.

We at the agency have come to predict which candidates will receive not one, but many offers. We have analyzed what characteristics each of these candidates possesses, exactly what is the common denominator that produces success. It is, first and foremost, the ability to create a splendid first impression which projects a great deal of honesty, sincerity, and enthusiasm. Given several candidates with virtually identical credentials, the job offer invariably will be made to the person who seems most interested and enthusiastic about the job.

Creating the Right Impression

Because the very first impression you make will carry through the entire interview and greatly determine its outcome, it is imperative to create the best impression possible.

Your appearance, the way you are dressed, your attitude, and the way you communicate nonverbally are basically what determine the impression you make.

How do you convey the impression of sincerity? Easy!! By being honest, open, and real. Be yourself. Take the attitude the company wants to see you and feel confident. This starts the self-fulfilling prophecy. Feel successful and chances are you will be successful.

Any form of role-playing that projects a personality other than your own is bound to lead to a disastrous interview. There is no way to predict what kind of person the employer is looking for, and if, in fact you knew, it is highly unlikely you could keep up the drama for the duration of the interview. Not only should you avoid trying to be "cool" but you should shun any "persona" that is not your own. Be yourself! Walking into an interview with this intention will be the first step toward losing the interview "jitters." Knowing that you will be hired for your qualifications and for your personality, *just as they are*, goes a long way toward making you appear an interested and sincere prospect.

By enthusiasm, we don't mean bubbling, ingenuous radiance. On the other hand, we do not mean—very definitely do not mean—a "cool," detached, attitude. Any attempt to be "cool" can easily be interpreted as boredom, apathy, or even antagonism on your part, and such attitudes inevitably lead to a rapid, and unsatisfactory, termination of the interview. A simple way of showing interest is to look back on the research you have done on the company before the interview. Furthermore, if the information you obtained on the firm impressed *you* favorably, it has a tendency to "psych you up," to make you *want* to get that particular job, and that, in itself, will come out as enthusiasm as you are interviewed. Enthusiasm indicates not only interest but a high energy level. Employers feel high-energy people not only will get the job done, but will inspire staff members to "get moving." It is not unusual for employers who have interviewed several candidates referred by our agency to call us to help make the decision which person to hire. After some discussion, we always find the employer almost invariably chooses to offer the job to the person who seems most enthusiastic.

Even though we discussed it earlier, we cannot overestimate the importance of being as completely honest during your interview as you were in writing your résumé. True, it is tempting to exaggerate, distort, delete, tell a tiny white lie or half-truth, say anything to make ourselves seem a little better than we are, but anyone who does this is playing with fire. Once caught in a lie, no matter how slight, you lose all credibility and can seriously damage your reputation.

Another reason for being completely honest is that it is easier. If you depart from the truth on your job application, résumé, or interview, you are putting an additional load on your memory and this will serve to increase your apprehension. The interviewer expects some nervousness on your part and usually will try to dispel it. However, if your nervousness increases as the interview continues, this can be interpreted as an indication that you are afraid of being found in a lie.

In a sense, your employment is an unspoken contract between you and the company. There is a mutual benefit which both parties agree to after assessing the facts available to them. Either party would be justified in cancelling this unspoken contract if the other party had falsified any of the information. If you accepted a job at a low salary because of a promise of a sizable increase after three months employment, you would feel you had been treated unfairly if you didn't get the raise when the time arrived. And, conversely, your employer is equally justified in cancelling the contract if you had been hired as a result of false information.

It is not merely a matter of morality; hiring and "breaking in" a new employee is an expensive process for a company. In addition to the clerical costs involved in setting up a personnel file, adding to the insurance roster, setting up payroll cards, etc., there is also the fact that many offices feel that few employees can *earn* their salary until having worked for the company for at least three months. One of the functions of the personnel department of any company is the avoidance of any such *unnecessary* expenses. For that, among other reasons, it is best to be direct, cordial, and always honest in all your replies.

Always keep in mind a feeling of equality between you and your interviewer. Being too humble or subservient is as bad as being too arrogant. Never say you'll take anything; that gives an impression of desperation and furthermore, you *won't* take anything. (Honestly, would you *really* sweep the floors or file all day?) If the interviewer asks you what kind of job you are looking for, answer in terms of a job title—accountant, Gal/Guy Friday, Secretary, Media Trainee, Sales or Marketing trainee, Management trainee. Saying "I don't know" is the kiss of death. The interviewer's response to that answer is "If you don't know, how should I know?" And the interview is quickly terminated.

Be a good listener, but feel free to ask questions. Be sure, however, that the questions are pertinent and will indicate interest in joining forces with the employer conducting the interview. Take advantage of any pause in the conversation to ask related questions yourself, to be sure you have as complete a picture as possible of the position open, the company objectives, and the part you would play in them. Usually the interviewer will ask you if you have any questions. Remember, you will also be judged by what you ask.

Be careful about asking for guarantees. Asking where the job will lead cannot truthfully be answered in an interview. Only after you are employed can the employer honestly evaluate your talents and potentials. If the company offers you—a college grad—a job, you can be sure it is one with career potential. Employers are aware that college grads will not do well or stay in a dead-end job, and, not wanting unnecessary turnover, usually will only offer degree-holders those positions offering upward mobility. However, during the interview, it is impossible to predict where your talents and interests can be used most fully. After working in the company a short time, you and your supervisor will decide what department will offer the maximum challenge. You might find, however, though your heart was originally set on a career in editorial marketing, sales, public relations, personnel, advertising, or market research might be much more satisfying.

Always be flexible about salary and be willing to think in terms of the potential salary being offered. At the start of your career, what you can learn, where the job might lead, the chemistry between you and your supervisor, the company benefits are equally as important as the starting salary.

If you are offered the job, love it and have nothing else pending, by all means, accept it. However, if you have gone on other interviews and are waiting for a decision, simply tell the interviewer you appreciate the offer, and are seriously considering it, and will call in a few days with a decision.

Even if you don't get the job, you must not dismiss the interview as time wasted. As a neophyte in the job market, at least you have experienced an interview and found out that it was not as terrifying as you had anticipated. You probably did make a good impression even though you didn't land the job. It is more than likely your résumé and application will be filed and you may be considered for another opening in the near future. This last is a very common occurrence; at our agency we often get calls asking if one of our applicants we had sent to an account weeks ago was still available for work.

Remember, the interviewer is trying very hard to find a really well-qualified, dependable person to fill the present opening. With this in mind, you must convince the interviewer that it is in the best interest of the employer to hire you. You must present yourself in such a manner that the interviewer will feel your assets, talents, and qualifications are far superior to any other candidate.

Be Prepared

There is a skill involved in interviewing and, like any other skill, it can be easily learned and once acquired, will serve you well during your working life.

Quite simply it is this: *come prepared*. Learn as much as possible about the company where you are being interviewed. If it's an ad agency, find out who their accounts are; if a publisher, what they publish: textbooks, trade books, magazines, etc. Find out what are the company's main products, services, or specialties. Learn who are their executives, directors, or partners, the number of employees, branch offices, and any information concerning acquisitions or mergers.

This information is not as esoteric as one would believe. All of this information can be obtained in your local library. Your library contains business directories covering every field. Such directories as *Standard & Poor's* (business), *Dun & Bradstreet, F & J Index of Corporations and Industries* (self-explanatory), *Martindale Hubbell* (law firms), *Literary Market Place* (publishing), *Standard Directory of Advertising Agencies* (advertising) offer a wealth of material.

The second step of being prepared is thinking through your *verbal* résumé. Your verbal résumé consists of facts and information not included in the written one—such as salary requirements. It is more than likely the interviewer will ask you about your salary requirements. When discussing your present minimum salary, try to be quite open. If you know what salary is being offered, be sure your salary expectations are in that range. Remember, the interview is a screening process and if your minimum salary is considerably higher than the employer intends to pay, you'll automatically be eliminated as a candidate. Ironically, often the actual salary offered is quite a bit higher than the original salary listed, so it is imperative to keep in the running.

Let the interviewer know that the starting salary is not your only consideration; you're just as concerned about other conditions. You might consider a lower salary if there is a good chance for advancement, the job offers unusual challenge, or the employer is enjoying a period of rapid growth. This basic philosophy is simply: get a job offer. Only after the offer can you negotiate a higher salary.

An important step of "being prepared" or "doing your homework" is so simple that it's often overlooked. *Reread* your résumé. The interviewer will probably have a copy of your résumé before him or her and it is quite likely that a reference will be made to specific sections that need clarification or expansion. The interviewer might refer to one summer job and if you haven't looked at a copy of your résumé for a time, there is a good chance you'll founder while trying to remember which summer you worked where. Unfortunately, not having the facts at your fingertips might cause you to lose some credibility.

Questions and Answers

How often have you thought, after an exam in college, "If I knew what questions they were going to ask, I could have done better"? Because that's such a universal feeling, we asked well over a thousand personnel interviewers to tell us what kind of questions they usually ask an entry-level college grad. Though every interview is different, all will include a group of questions which you will be expected to answer in a poised, articulate manner without fumbling. The interviewer will not only be listening to your answers, but will be judging your knowledge, self-confidence, poise, and ability to think quickly.

Knowing beforehand what kinds of questions are likely to be asked and thinking about the answers you will give will be very helpful in giving a strong impression of yourself on your interview. It is a good idea to spend enough time to do a bit of soul-searching and develop answers to the following questions. Of course, the questions are merely representative; *all* will not be asked, but we can bet a few will. Say the questions out loud to a friend, husband, wife, relative, or even a tape recorder:

1. Where do you expect to be in five years?
2. What are your short-range goals?
3. What are your long-range goals?
4. Why did you choose _____ college or university?

5. I see you are Phi Beta Kappa; did you spend most of your time studying?
6. What did you enjoy most in your summer jobs?
7. What did you enjoy least in your summer jobs?
8. What do you consider to be your outstanding achievement?
9. Why did you have such a low average in college?
10. Do you work well under pressure?
11. How do you feel about excessive overtime?
12. Do you work well with other people?
13. Do you prefer to work alone?
14. Do you enjoy solving problems?
15. How often have you been ill in the past five years?
16. Are you willing to take a battery of tests such as physical, personality, intelligence, aptitude, or psychological?
17. What do you consider your greatest strength?
18. What do you consider your greatest weakness?
19. Are you willing to relocate?
20. Are you willing to travel?
21. What was your average in grade school, college, law school, medical school?
22. Did you work while you were in college?
23. How was your education financed?
24. What newspapers do you read?
25. How do you like to spend your free time?
26. Were you involved in extra-curricular activities? If so, what?
27. What magazines do you read on a more or less regular basis?
28. Tell me a little about your hobbies.
29. Why do you want to work for this company?
30. Are you married or engaged?
31. What is your minimum salary?
32. What talents do you possess that you think would be beneficial to this company?
33. Can you explain what motivates you?
34. What is your definition of success?

There is no *right* answer to these questions. Each person will answer them differently. Don't try to figure out what would be an impressive answer and make that your own; that kind of "phoniness" is very obvious to an experienced interviewer and is bound to create a very negative impression.

Before you can interview successfully, you must know something that everyone in personnel knows but rarely is apparent to the uninitiated in the dynamics of the hiring process. The job offer is not usually made to the *most* qualified candidate or the person with the highest average, but rather to the applicant who *best creates the impression* that he or she cannot only do the job very successfully, but, by the demonstration of the honesty and enthusiasm projected, will be a great asset to the company.

The Total Picture

Be prompt. Lateness is rude, is inconsiderate of the interviewer's time, and is guaranteed to get the interview to a bad start. It's a good idea not to overload when setting up appointments for interviews. We suggest no more than one interview in the morning and one in the afternoon. There is no way of predicting just how long an interview will last, and you shouldn't put yourself under the additional pressure of trying to keep another appointment.

Dress appropriately, which means don't overdress or underdress. Dress more or less as if you were already part of the staff.

If, however, you're applying for a job in a field such as design, publishing, art, etc., where the atmosphere is extremely informal and anything goes (dungarees, jeans, overalls, etc.), you still should dress in conservative business clothes. A chemist should not apply for a position in a lab coat or a nurse in a uniform. Interviewing is serious business and one should dress appropriately.

With very few exceptions, dressing appropriately means a suit for a man, and a conservative dress, suit, sweater, skirt and blouse (sweater), or possibly a pantsuit for a woman. Your clothes should be neat and clean, shoes polished (and comfortable; don't ever even try breaking in new shoes when going out on interviews), have nails well groomed, and women should avoid using very dark or bright nail polish or heavy makeup.

Do's and Don'ts

There is much else to tell you, but we feel as college graduates, you are bright enough to not mention the obvious. You know you shouldn't pick your teeth or file your nails, chew gum, or bite your nails. Advice like that you don't need. You're too intelligent and our belaboring such suggestions would be talking down to you. Below is a simplified list of the do's and don'ts of the interview.

- Don't arrange for more than one interview in the morning and one in the afternoon.
- Do be prompt at the appointed time. Arriving late is discourteous, inconsiderate, and is guaranteed to create hostility and hence an unfavorable interview. If for any reason you are delayed, phone and reschedule the interview as soon as possible.
- Do smile when you greet the interviewer. Give a firm "connecting" handshake.
- Do greet the interviewer by name. If you don't know his or her name, ask the receptionist. Be certain that you have the correct pronunciation.
- Do fill out the application forms in their entirety even if the information asked is already in your résumé.
- Do try to appear poised and alert. Make sure your clothing, aside from being professional, is comfortable, and try to seat yourself in as relaxed a manner as possible without sprawling.
- Don't answer questions with a simple "yes" or "no." Rather, reply with a brief, concise explanation. Don't over-answer.

- Do ask questions. If there are aspects of the job that are not clear to you, ask. Whether your questions concern duties or benefits, you certainly have a right to know.
- Don't try to interview the interviewer. Trying to dominate the interview may give you a feeling of self-assurance, but it won't get you the job.
- Do be sure that the interviewer is aware of your strong points in a straightforward, factual manner. Again, keep it brief.
- Don't ask at the first opportunity what the paid holidays and vacations are. You don't want to give the impression that your prime interest is how little work you will be doing.
- Do be flexible. The philosophy is to get as many job offers as possible, and then choose the best.
- Don't be downhearted. The failure to get a job from an interview doesn't mean that you are a failure. There are other jobs, other interviews. Besides, you need only one job. One of our mottoes at the agency is "Discouragement is a luxury you cannot afford."
- Do be polite at all times. Should the interviewer do anything to provoke your hostility, keep it under wraps until you get out.
- Don't hide. Some people try to hide their nervousness by hiding parts of themselves. Mannerisms such as covering the mouth while talking or wearing sunglasses create negative impressions.
- Do try for eye-to-eye contact. Looking "someone straight in the eye" is a fine way to establish rapport. Avoiding eye contact can be interpreted as being evasive and indirect.
- Do phone soon after the interview. Saying "thank you" will help the interviewer to remember you.

You may get the offer at the interview, or it may not come until later. One week after the interview, phone back and ask if you are still "at bat." Never try to push an employer into a decision by saying you've been offered another job (unless, of course, it is true). The employer will always advise you to take the other job, even if you were being actively considered. The employer doesn't want to take the responsibility of your losing out on another offer, and if he or she thinks you are attempting to be manipulative, it will lead only to resentment—not to a job offer.

Final Thoughts

By now you know how to write an arresting, interview-getting résumé; how to go about your job hunt; how to survive an interview; and how to follow up. Aside from phone calls, there are other methods of follow-up that will increase your chances of getting the job.

Remember the competition. They are probably all entry-level college graduates with pretty much the same credentials so the employer is having a hard time making a decision. And often it really is a toss-up. The correct follow-up letter can often provide that extra push to get you in the company's door.

The Magic Power of Enthusiasm

A follow-up letter can help because it provides the magic power of enthusiasm. Employment counselors usually agree that the most enthusiastic person gets the job in a toss-up. So why not provide the enthusiasm? It can only help.

The best way to follow up is to say "thank you." You may want to say it to the person who told you about a job, to let the person know that you appreciate the effort; or you may want to thank the interviewer, letting him or her know of your enthusiasm. The letter will keep your image fresh in the person's mind. And that's definitely a plus! Read the sample letters beginning on page 147. The first two are thank-yous, both to the interviewer and to the person who might have gotten you the interview.

Even "after the fact," it pays to follow up. For example, you've been offered a job, and have accepted it. But you are presently working and have just given your employer two weeks' notice. A simple confirmation, accepting the job and thanking the person who's hiring you, will reassure your immediate supervisor-to-be that he or she has made the right decision; it may also assure you of a warmer reception two weeks hence when you show up for the first day on the job.

The confirmation should be simply written. Just confirm the fact that you have accepted the job, tell how happy you are to have it, and confirm the date on which you will report to start the job.

Other Follow-Ups

If you went on an interview and, because you were told your typing wasn't good enough, you increased your skill both in speed and accuracy, it is very important to call the interviewer and give him or her this information. This knowledge not only will increase your qualifications but shows unusual motivation and again, enthusiasm.

Also, it is not unusual for a neophyte job hunter, when on an interview, to ask for a higher salary than is realistic, and, is for that reason not considered as a candidate. If you made that mistake and now would take a lower salary, by all means, call the interviewer and give him or her this new information. It might put you back "in the running" and even land you the job.

"No Thank You, but..."

You have been offered a job, but for one reason or another you have refused it. It's an awkward situation that can be made smoother by a follow-up letter, especially if you are interested in working for the company, perhaps at some future time, or maybe in some other capacity that you have decided would better suit you.

Just let them know why you're refusing. Maybe you have accepted another job, but are unsure that it will work out satisfactorily. Then, letting them know will be a way of keeping your options open. If the company was interested enough in you to offer you a job at that time, it is quite possible that they will be happy to consider you for a job at some future time, providing the situation is mutually satisfactory. In other words, you are saying, "No thank you, but...," and who knows when your letter might pay off in the future. It's apt to make a good impression for your courtesy alone. Companies like to think they are worth your time and effort, especially when they have extended any courtesies to you. And, of course, they are worth it!

On page 150 is a sample letter to illustrate what kind of letters we recommend. They are only suggestions, and your particular situation, plus your ingenuity, will dictate exactly what type of letter to write.

Which Job Do I Take?

You've worked hard, you've spent weeks on the job hunt, and finally you've bagged your quarry: two or three job offers. Now you have a new problem. Your thoughts change from "How do I get a job I would like?" to "Which job shall I accept?" Your first impulse, if your reactions are similar to the thousands of college graduates our agency has placed, sounds easy. The one that offers the highest salary! Well, maybe yes and maybe no. There is more to be considered than money.

As a recent college graduate your priorities are somewhat different from someone half way up the corporate ladder. Does this job offer actually give what you want? If the job requires relocation, do you really want to relocate? If you are married or engaged, how would this relocation affect that person? Have you thought about the cost of living in a different city? Remember, to judge the worth of your salary properly, it must be compared to the cost of living. What are the cultural activities in the new city? And how important are they to you? Do you think you might feel uprooted? Is it easy for you to plant new seeds? If the job doesn't work out, would you be stuck in the middle of nowhere or are there other companies in the area where you might find work?

All of the above require a great deal of honest self-study, and you must be quite convinced that you really can handle relocation before actually accepting an offer. Because of that, sometimes companies offer higher salaries on hard-to-fill jobs (extremely bad locations or working conditions, or a "no potential" or dead-end job, a situation that allows for no personal growth, limited company benefits, etc.).

Think through some of your personal needs. You've just come to a large metropolis and you don't know *anybody*. You've just received two job offers. In one, the higher-paid of the two, you'll be working in a small office with one or two other people; in the other with 7 percent less pay, you'll be a member of a large staff and have the opportunity to meet lots of people.

Since you've come to the city to start a new life, you must consider a job that offers an opportunity to expand your social life as something more valuable to you than money.

Some companies provide training programs; others are willing to pay part (or all) of the costs of any education (university courses or private schools) that will increase your skills and knowledge. How valuable is that to you? What is it worth? How will additional education help you in the future? Do any of the companies offering you a position have this policy? Certainly worth considering.

How much you can learn in a particular job should be a very serious consideration, too. Not only is your future marketability very dependent on the knowledge, skills, and certain know-how you gain on your first job, but you'll probably be happier in an atmosphere where you can continue to grow. Think in terms of what your college education cost in dollars and cents and now measure the value of a job, where not only can you learn, but are paid for doing it. In many cases, a year's experience in a certain job is worth more than a Master's Degree.

Another consideration should be which company and it's position will be the most impressive on your résumé. Not that you're thinking of changing jobs before you start, but let's face it, this is no longer the time where people stay on a job all of their lives. People usually make at least five job changes in their working life and might even make one or two major career changes.

Be sure when making your decision, that you have considered the importance of being happy. My agency advises entry-level job seekers to take the job they instinctively feel good about, the job where the chemistry is "right," where they feel the most comfortable. We've found being happy in a job guarantees better job performance and hence promotion. We've also found that most companies promote from within and will always consider their staff members before they start recruiting for a new job opportunity. We've mentioned our philosophy before, but feel it is important enough to bear repetition. "Proximity is the mother of opportunity." The "wrong" job in the right company can quickly become the "right" job in the right company.

Just as job searching is a thinking process, so is job selection. There is much to think about in selecting a job offer. It is never solved by simply flipping a coin. You must try to really think about *you*, and in which job you think your skills, talents, and special abilities will be used to the most advantage—where *you* will be the happiest. Don't make the mistake of "overthinking," which we guarantee will end you in confusion.

And once you make the decision, stick to it and commit yourself completely. Getting the job is the first and very important step. Your next goal should be making the job your job. By giving it your all and approaching it with integrity and imagination, you will change that job into a challenging career.

July 8, 1984

Mr. Martin Severance
Marketing Director
Smith & Smith, Inc.
68 Meeker Street
Oakland, California 94610

Dear Mr. Severance:

I just wanted to write to you to tell you
how much I enjoyed and appreciated meeting with
you last Wednesday. Thank you for the time you
spent with me and for considering me for the
position as your assistant. The job is exactly
what I am looking for. Should I get it, I will
prove I have much to offer your company.

I will call next week, hoping for a positive
decision.

Sincerely,

Jane Robbins

May 6, 1984

Miss Sheila McBride
28 Grey Place
Boston, Mass. 02145

Dear Sheila:

Thank you so much for referring me to Mr. Donald Moore at the Coors Research Company. He is just as nice as you described him, and he interviewed me for a job as a Market Research Trainee.

I think I made a good impression, and the job sounds fabulous. I would start as a Guy Friday and be trained to do research: exactly what I am looking for.

I'm to call Mr. Moore next week to set up a second interview. My fingers are crossed.

In any case, Sheila, I want to thank you for taking the time to give me this great lead. I'll let you know what happens as soon as I know.

Regards to your family and special greetings to your husband.

Sincerely,

David

June 16, 1984

Ms. Diane Oxman
Media Director
Hamilton Advertising Company
Boston, Massachusetts 22117

Dear Ms. Oxman:

I am delighted to confirm my acceptance of the job as Media Assistant. I am available to start work at the time you specified, and I look forward to seeing you Monday morning, July 1.

Let me say again how happy I am at getting the job and how much I look forward to working with you. I feel it is the perfect job for me and you can be sure I expect to give it "my all."

Until July 1, I am

Sincerely,

Alice Greysmith

August 27, 1984

Mrs. Marian Bell
Art Director
Capital Records
Rockland, Connecticut 06013

Dear Mrs. Bell:

I'm really sorry that I had to tell you that I couldn't accept your job offer as an Art Trainee. It sounded like a great opportunity, but just yesterday I accepted a position with a pattern company. I'm really sorry because I am still very impressed with Capital Records and feel I would very likely fit in well with your staff.

As I am not at all sure how my new job is going to work out, will you please be kind enough to keep my application on file, and contact me if there is another opening in the next few months? May I please call you should my position not work out?

Thank you for your offer, and again, I am sorry I have to refuse it.

Cordially,

Nancy Feldman

Appendix

Record-Keeping Blanks

Keep a record of each résumé sent and note the dates of your calls and interviews. Also indicate the results of each call and interview, and remember your follow-up letters. Don't leave anything to your memory; maintain a written record.

The simplest way of maintaining a record of your direct mail campaign, answers to classified ads, or résumés mailed through personal contacts is to make a carbon copy of each covering letter as you type it. On the bottom of the carbon, you can note date and result of your follow-up phone call, date of interview, result of interview, and follow-up note. These can be kept in a file folder with a separate sheet—or calendar page—with dates and times of interviews noted. It would be disastrous to set up two interviews for the same time.

A second system is to set up a large sheet of paper with column headings across the top of the sheet. The information, of course, would be the same as that maintained by using carbon copies. Below is the suggested heading for each column. The headings would be separated by lines drawn vertically down the full length of the sheet, and horizontal lines would be drawn, each about two inches below the other, to separate the entries for each company written. I suggest the following headings:

Résumé Mailing	Follow-Up Phone Call	Interview	Thank-You Letter	Job Offer	Confirmation or "No Thank You, But" Letter
Name	Date	Date	Date	Yes	Date
Title	Results	Time		No	Letter Type
Company	_____	Interviewer			
Address	_____	Results			
_____		_____			
_____		_____			
Date Sent		_____			
		_____			

The third system involves the use of 4 × 6-inch index cards. Again, the information would be the same as the other systems. Below is a sample layout for the card:

Mr. Richard Rowe   Mailed 3/22/84
Chief Draftsman
Systems, Inc.
424 Park Place
Buford, Pa. 21370

Phone Call: _____
                                    (indicate date)

(Note results) _____

Interview: _____
                        (indicate date, time, and interviewer)

(Note results) _____

Thank-You Letter _____
                                    (indicate date)

Job Offer _____

Confirmation or "No Thank You, But" Letter _____
                                        (indicate date and letter type)

This system is best for a very large mailing. We suggest that you have the index cards printed up cheaply rather than trying to type them yourself.

Keeping a record of your job campaign is worth the effort it takes. Especially when you are involved with a large mailing, it is the only way of insuring that you will be able to keep track of which companies you have contacted and what the results were. Aside from eliminating the chances of sending a résumé to the same company twice, or of making two interview appointments for the same time, it provides a useful means of reviewing the progress of your job campaign at any given time.

Card 1

Résumé Mailing

Name _____

Title _____

Company _____

Address _____
_____

Date Sent _____

Follow-Up Phone Call

Date _____

Results _____
_____

Interview

Date _____

Time _____

Interviewer _____

Results _____

Thank-You Letter

Date _____

Job Offer

Yes _____

No _____

Confirmation or "No Thank You, But" Letter

Date _____

Letter Type _____

Card 2

Résumé Mailing

Name _____

Title _____

Company _____

Address _____
_____

Date Sent _____

Follow-Up Phone Call

Date _____

Results _____
_____

Interview

Date _____

Time _____

Interviewer _____

Results _____

Thank-You Letter

Date _____

Job Offer

Yes _____

No _____

Confirmation or "No Thank You, But" Letter

Date _____

Letter Type _____

Job Search Check-List

Now that we have discussed the various steps to be taken in your search for the "perfect" job, and you are either ready to begin that search or are already in the midst of it, use the check-off list below to make sure that you have explored all the possible methods of job hunting.

DID YOU . . .

1. Determine that you want to begin/change your career.
2. Analyze your skills, talents, and past accomplishments.
3. Explore different fields through library research, peer discussion, and employment counseling.
4. Target an objective.
5. Prepare a résumé inventory.
6. Compose a résumé and have it typed and printed.
7. Investigate help wanted ads (classified newspapers and trade journals).
8. Check out contacts.
9. Research potential employers in business reference section of local library.
10. Consider using an employment agency.
11. Determine ads, companies, contacts you wish to forward your résumé to.
12. Begin direct mail campaign by writing appropriate cover letter to accompany résumé.
13. Mail résumé and cover letter to targeted list of top 25 choices.
14. Record names and maintain complete files of mailing list, including when sent, whom to, what for, and all responses.
15. Prepare for potential interviews — determine what you want to say about yourself, get necessary portfolios, etc. together, prepare/buy an appropriate interview outfit.
16. Secure the interview.
17. Interview.
18. Send follow-up thank you note.
19. Find out how you did (telephone call).
20. *Negative* — begin step 11 again with new targets.
    Positive — job offer.
21. Ask potential employer any questions omitted during initial interview.
22. Negotiate salary.
23. Decide which offers to accept.
24. Accept offer.
25. Embark on your "perfect job."